Never Light a Match in the Outhouse

Funny Stories from Cottage Country

Edited by Matt Jackson
Summit Studios

Library and Archives Canada Cataloguing in Publication

Never light a match in the outhouse : funny stories
from cottage country / edited by Matt Jackson.

Issued in print and electronic formats.
ISBN 978-0-9866856-6-8 (pbk.).--ISBN 978-0-9866856-8-2 (pdf).--
ISBN 978-0-9866856-7-5 (html)

1. Vacation homes--Humor. 2. Vacations--Humor.
3. Country life--Humor. 4. Canadian wit and humor (English).
I. Jackson, Matt, editor

PN6231.C65N48 2014   C818'.60208   C2014-903982-4
                                                 C2014-903983-2

Designed by Kirk Seton, Signet Design Inc.
Cover illustration © 2014 David Banks
Printed and bound in Canada

SUMMIT STUDIOS
3022 Washington Ave.
Victoria, British Columbia V9A 1P6

This book is dedicated to all those

who love cottage country.

Table of Contents

Introduction

By Matt Jackson

It's rare that you'll meet a Canadian who hasn't experienced a defining moment in cottage country. Whether it's memories from a childhood spent swimming, fishing or picking berries at the lake, making S'mores or toasting marshmallows around the cottage campfire, or simply laying out on the dock and watching the stars appear one after another, I think it's fair to say there's a collective cottaging experience that almost every Canadian can relate to.

One of my own memorable moments happened at my grandparents' cottage on Wizard Lake, a lake about an hour southwest of Edmonton that lies in a deep glacial trough. I was about twelve years old at the time, and I was there alone with my grandparents Bill and Norma Baird. We had been passing the time in usual splendid fashion: paddling their canoe out to fishing spots during the day, working on the latest building project, and reading stories to each other around the indoor fireplace. On one particularly sunny day, my grandpa suggested we take the motorboat down to The Point, which was one of the lake's prime swimming spots. We all thought it was a great idea, so my grandma packed a picnic lunch for our adventure.

From what I can recall, it took about a half hour to reach The Point. The sun was shining, the water was warm, and after eating a scrumptious meal that probably included such things as salmon sandwiches, dill pickles, homemade cookies and deviled eggs, we enjoyed a luxurious swim in water that dropped off steeply from the sandy shoreline. After we'd had our fill, we took out three inflatable inner tubes so that we could lounge on top of them and nap with our hats pulled across our faces. It was the kind of peaceful scene that anybody who spends time in cottage country will be familiar with.

It wasn't long before two of us were snoring softly—fully immersed in the serenity of our surroundings. The other one of us (I'm not going to say who), was having some trouble sitting still. Mischief was running through his head, until finally, a duplicitous idea emerged.

I slipped ever so quietly off my tube and into the lake. Somewhere in the background the theme song from *Jaws* was playing as I knifed through the water toward my unsuspecting grandfather. When I was about three feet away from him, I ducked my head underwater, and a few seconds later came up directly beneath his inner tube.

It must have been a spectacular sight: my grandfather's limbs flailing in every direction as he pitched backwards—his feet rotating high over his head—and into the drink.

When the coughing and sputtering had ceased, I saw something in my grandfather's eyes that I had never seen before. Normally, he was the kindest and most peace loving of men. But I swear in those eyes—for the briefest of instants, at least—I glimpsed the silver flash of a guillotine dropping toward my tingling neck.

"Matthew!" he spluttered. "What in the name of...?!"

"Grandpa ... I'm sorry. I'm really, really sorry!"

By that evening—and for many years after—we were able to laugh about the incident. Still, for years to come, I did notice that my grandfather would stay awake and alert whenever we were playing in or near the water.

This collection of stories is intended to celebrate the cottage country experience with laughter and good humor. A wide variety of authors have written to us with their best yarns, almost all of them true. Even those stories which perhaps take a few liberties with the facts—such as David Jones's ode to cottage relaxation—do so in the spirit of telling a good story. Is there such a thing as relaxing *too* much at the cottage? Jones doesn't think so, as he relates in his prize-winning ode to sloth titled "Lazy Lake."

There are of course the requisite tales about boating, including "Cape Tormentine" by Bob Dixon, which describes several exciting escapades at his family's cottage in New Brunswick. Reading it made me wonder how he and his friends survived their youth. There are also a few stories about fishing—both on good days and bad—including one incident where Jeff Groberman was extremely grateful that the fish at the end of his line managed to get away. His story, which is titled "Moby Dick," is one of the most unbelievable tales that I heard while assembling this anthology. And he swears that it's true!

We've naturally included a few stories about run-ins with the wildlife: bears, porcupines, muskrats and mink. And crocodiles. Yes, you read that correctly: crocodiles in Ontario's cottage country! Courtesy of Alex Hamilton-Brown.

James Osborne has a pair of stories in the book. In one, you will meet a golfer who loses his mind, and in the other, a practical joker who has the best (or worst) practical joke played on him by his cottage neighbors who are absolutely salivating to "get him good."

We've even included a story about two newlyweds, written by Michelle Bland-Bruce, who spent a winter living at a remote Alaskan camp trapping animals and living off the land. It's an experience that delivered a few surprises, but in the end was precisely the adventure the young couple had been yearning for.

I hope you enjoy reading these stories as much as I did collecting and editing them. The diversity of outdoor writing talent we have in Canada always amazes me, and it's exciting when a project like this comes to fruition. Enshrined by way of paper and ink, these tales now have a much better chance of being remembered and appreciated for generations to come.

Lazy Lake

A place where procrastination reigns supreme.

By David Jones

The sun had slipped over the forested hills and the reflected sky in the lake was a blur of red, orange, and pink. My old buddy Pauly and I pulled our jackets on and sank back into our chairs to reminisce about the soon ending summer.

"Ya know, Pauly, it doesn't seem so long ago that you and I put that dock in and soon we'll be haulin' it out."

"Well, it was actually just a few weeks ago that we got around to it. Remember?"

"No way! Seems a lot longer than that. Didn't really use it much—ya think we should just leave it in for next year?"

"Sounds good to me."

We clinked beer bottles and horsed back a good swig. Then we fell silent as the ghostly call of a loon echoed across the darkening waters.

I broke the quiet. "The Canada Day barbecue was a good one this year, eh? Lotta folks liked the real charcoal flavor of the burgers."

"Yeah. Turned out real good. Too bad we ran outta propane— but you really saved the day by filling the Weber with charcoal, buddy. Mind you, it'll be a helluva mess to clean if you're ever gonna use propane again."

"That's true, but ya know what they say: 'Let sleeping dogs lie.'"

"Yup. Fer sure. But fix those wacky boards on the front porch, eh?"

Aunt Bunny had come over for the fireworks on the May long weekend and had strolled across the porch to admire the Jumbo Powder Keg Fountain as its eight colors of crackles, stars, and torches lit the sky for three full minutes. When she stepped back to take a pull on her lemonade, she'd had the misfortune of hitting the "lucky spot" and her right leg had snapped through the board. Now, Aunt Bunny is a certain size and she was wedged in there pretty good—and for quite awhile too, because we couldn't hear her over the fireworks. We finally fetched the engine hoist from the shed and pulled her out. But she was some upset because her lemonade had spilled.

"Oh, no sense doin' it now. Maybe you can come over and we can give the old place a going over in the spring. We'll fix anything that needs it."

"Sure, be glad to. But how come we never got anything done this spring?"

"Geez, don't you remember? It rained the weekend we were really fired up, then the next few weekends were so nice, we just sat right here fishin'."

"Hey! You remember the night ol' Garney from down the road went in the outhouse and sneezed while he was takin' a leak? Ha! Blew his false teeth right down the hole. Thought I was gonna die!"

"Ha! Dopey old fart shoulda just gone in the bush like everyone else."

"Yeah ... especially bein' the Beer 'n' Baked Bean Banquet. Whew..."

There *had* been a few difficulties over the summer, but why do people own cottages? To relax, right? Who wants to jockey through traffic for hours and then spend the weekend doing maintenance? My wife Mary agrees. Don't see her much at the cottage. She spends most of the summer doing two-thousand-piece jigsaw puzzles, or lounging in the old rocker on the safe side of the porch reading romance novels.

"What ya think the chances are of Buck bringin' his boat up again next year?"

I wagged my head. "Not too good, I'd say. He left in a pretty big huff."

"Yeah. Bit of a crybaby, ain't he?" Pauly chuckled.

"Well, he did have a point. The ding he got on the prop made a heck of a vibration. Totally spoiled the fishing, truth be told."

"That was his fault. We told him to crank the motor up high."

"Yeah, we truly did. The boat floatin' away was completely his doing too—he didn't tie it up properly. He shouldn't have complained, though: I sent Mary to swim out and fetch the boat back. Actually, *I'm* ticked that he ripped up the lawn tryin' to haul that barge out. Truck dug into the grass almost to its axles for Pete's sake. Then he groused when we winched the boat out and the cable snapped."

"Hooo. Didn't that windshield just smash to pieces? Nice groove on the hood, too. Maybe that's why he never offered to fix your winch."

"Oh, I don't really mind that. I was gonna replace that cable years ago after Jimmy nipped it with his metal cutting tool. I'm just miffed that Buck left those ruts in the lawn. You know, Mary twisted her ankle pretty bad when she was takin' the empty two-fours to the shed."

The night had cooled off. We needed to fend off the chill. I hollered for Mary and ordered two brandies and two more beers. There was no response.

"She's probably deep in some romance novel. Want me to get them?"

"Nah. I'll be back in a minute. Get a fire goin' will you Pauly?"

I went in. Mary was in the living room slumped over on the couch with puzzle pieces covering the floor. An almost empty wine glass stood on the end table beside two empty bottles. Her snore was the kind you get here in cottage country. All that fresh air really cleans out your system and calms your soul. I poured the drinks and as I turned to take them outside, I stubbed my toe on the five-gallon pail on the floor. I made a mental note to empty it. Or maybe I should just fix the damn roof. I carefully nudged through the screen door so as not to wake Mary.

"Pauly, I thought you were makin' a fire?"

"The woodshed's empty. I thought you were gonna buy more wood?"

"Well, I was, but then I figured I'm surrounded by forest here—who needs to buy wood? I'll just go out and cut up some deadfall."

"Cool. What happened?"

"Oh, the chainsaw needs sharpening. Needs a bit of work too … it won't start. Say, why don't I go over to the shed and drag out the patio heater?"

"Good idea, man. Watch those ruts in the lawn."

The heater had worked its way to the back of the shed. I moved the water toys and broken lawn chairs and managed to dislodge it. There was an avalanche of beer cases. The heater felt heavy enough ... the tank seemed to be full. I dragged it out behind our chairs and lit it. A soft warmth came in welcome contrast to the cold night air. We sipped our brandies and hypothesized about the vastness of the universe and the meaning of life.

Then: *pop*.

"That didn't last very long. Was the tank full?"

"Dunno. Guess not or we woulda had propane for the barbecue, eh?"

Pauly shook his head, tossed down his brandy, guzzled his beer in one draught and got up.

"That's it, then. I'm outta here. We gonna haul the dock out tomorrow or leave it in?"

"Nah. There's still a few good weeks left."

Pauly's trail across the lawn was far from "as the crow flies," and he performed a masterful tuck and roll when he tripped over the large root that had popped out of the lawn. I made a mental note to sharpen the axe and take care of that soon. I wouldn't want Mary to get hurt haulin' empties again.

An incorrigible procrastinator, David Jones spent the latest cottage season catching up on chores of seasons past. Unfortunately, his deep devotion to relaxation caused most of those activities to be deferred for future consideration. You can read his blog at **www.thunderbridgeproductions.com**.

Small Boys with Slingshots

How to build a Weapon of Mashed Destruction.

By Don Wilkinson

There are a number of things boys shouldn't be exposed to before they reach a certain age. Say, forty. Just to be safe.

First on the list—after girls, I should say—is anything that explodes and/or shoots any type of projectile. This includes bows, arrows, shotguns, rifles, and of course that beloved favorite of Dennis the Menace, the slingshot!

For a few summers when I was a kid, my family rented a cottage on Aaron Lake near Southampton, Ontario. A farmer-type named Mr. McClellan had built four cottages on his property, and he rented them out to anyone dumb enough to want to rent a cottage on a small, turtle-infested lake. We were dumb enough to do so, and my brothers and I spent many happy hours catching turtles and stashing them in the waterlogged bottom of one of the cottage fishing boats. I have no idea what my sisters did.

Even catching turtles gets boring after a while, so my brother Dave and I sometimes wandered through the fields and up to the farm to see what was going on. One day, as we were walking through an old orchard, I felt the unmistakable *thwack!* of an apple hitting me broadside to the head. Strangely, it had come from the direction of my brother. I retaliated and soon apples were flying, which raised welts and left mushed apple bits in our hair, in our eyes, and even—mysteriously—inside our pants.

A ceasefire was called.

"You throw like a girl," I said.

The ceasefire ended.

Later, as we sat beneath the gnarled branches of an old apple tree, metaphorically licking our wounds, we discussed how we might build an "apple gun." We then noticed two branches of one particular tree that formed a perfect Y shape—not unlike a giant slingshot.

A quick search through the dusty junk piles reposing inside Farmer McClellan's tool shed produced several old inner tubes. We cut them into strips and knotted them together, which provided the perfect elastic implement that we needed to finish our weapon.

Dave scampered up the tree and tied the strips of tubing off. We then gathered armfuls of semi-rotten apples and readied our "Weapon of Mashed Destruction." Next, a target was picked on the old outhouse door about twenty meters away. Dave pulled the slingshot back and I placed a large ripe apple inside the pouch. Then he let go.

The giant rubber band went *twang!* as it snapped forward. The apple hurtled through the air at tremendous speed and vanished into a fine mist as it exploded against the outhouse door.

Dave and I glanced at each other. "Cooooool!"

Unbelievably, hurling apples at great speed against an outhouse can actually become boring. We glanced around for another target. Unfortunately, the farm dogs had long since disappeared and the cows were far out of range, even from our incredible weapon.

We set up another target against the sheep shed, about ten meters or so past the outhouse. But due to the additional forces and massive acceleration needed to reach it, the apples simply disintegrated in mid air. So we liberated some rocks from an old stone foundation wall instead. The first one sailed high over the shed roof and landed with a soft *sploosh* somewhere in the festering muck of the barnyard.

Ever larger rocks were chosen, and each traveled further than the last because we were hauling harder and harder on the slingshot.

Farmer McClellan's wife called from the front door to inform us that we should go back to our cottage. Luckily, we were in the backyard and chose not to hear her. At least, not until we had fired the largest rock of them all.

Dave and I pried a monstrous chunk of granite from the wall and carefully levered it into the sling. Digging in our heels, we managed to pull the slingshot back further and further until the very tree limbs were quivering from the strain. We released the rock and fell to the ground as the giant rubber bands snapped with enough force to slice our heads clean off had we been standing in the way.

We watched in awe as the rock sailed higher and higher and higher. It was with a kind of fascinated horror that we gradually realized we might have underestimated the velocity, trajectory, and distance of our final projectile. We stopped watching and carefully listened as the giant boulder—with a high-pitched and ominous whistle—vanished over the top of the farmhouse and out of sight.

A few milliseconds later we heard a very loud *crash!* We would later learn that the rock had punched clean through one wall of Farmer McClellan's barn, traversed the breadth of the hayloft, shattered several barn timbers as it passed through the far wall, and finally smashed into the tractor shed exactly ninety-seven feet from our launch point.

It was then that we decided to run!

Dave ran down to the cottage as fast as he could and lied to everyone who would listen that he had been there all day.

I ran out to the cornfield and hid among the stalks. I pretended not to hear the angry shouts from Farmer McClellan, his wife, my parents, and my oldest brother—who later admitted that he wished he'd been there to see the whole thing—and pretty much from everyone else who was at the farm.

Sadly, the next summer when we returned—yes, Farmer McClellan actually let us come back!—the old tree had been chopped down.

But the turtles were still there.

Don hasn't touched a slingshot since that memorable day; his wife won't let him near anything that shoots. Nowadays he teaches his grandkids how to do it instead, and then denies all knowledge if anything goes wrong. Wilkinson's story "Toyotas Don't Float" appeared in the Summit Studios anthology Never Trust a Smiling Bear *(2010).*

The Practical Joker

It's fair to say that he was surprised.

By Jim Osborne

Ken Hagerman was an incurable practical joker. When he and his wife Donna left a home after visiting, the host could be certain to find pictures hanging upside down, their bed short-sheeted or filled with kitchen utensils, or the toes of shoes stuffed with pebbles. And Ken was one of those special folks who also enjoyed practical jokes played on him. When someone got him good, he was the first to congratulate the perpetrator.

Of course, he would immediately begin plotting revenge.

Ken and Donna were neighbors in town. We were delighted when they also became neighbors at the lake—specifically Kootenay Lake near Crawford Bay, BC. During the summers that followed, we would often be at our cottages at the same time. It was on these occasions that practical jokes became almost daily events, much to the delight of our cottage neighbors and the chagrin of our spouses.

One year we were at our cottage midweek when Ken and Donna called to say they planned to be there by Friday afternoon. That wasn't unusual and we were looking forward to their arrival. But a couple of days later, Ken phoned again to say that they would be delayed until Saturday night.

Several of us immediately recognized this for what it was: a golden opportunity!

There were a few of us who jumped at the chance to get even for all the practical jokes Ken had played. We discussed various ideas and came up with a diabolical plot, one that would catch Ken completely by surprise. For once, we were confident that our plan would put us one-up on the undisputed King of Practical Jokes.

Here's how the plot unfolded. A year earlier, when Ken and Donna had bought their property, the previous owner had left behind a large roll of clear plastic shrink-wrap. An avid angler, Ken had used it to package freshly caught fish before freezing them. Other than that, the roll had been left untouched under the picnic table on Ken and Donna's deck.

The plot was a no-brainer. We were going to shrink wrap Ken and Donna's cottage.

We knew it would be dark when Ken and Donna arrived on Saturday night. They wouldn't notice until the last minute. With the shrink-wrap firmly in place, they'd be unable to open the door or to figure out how to get inside.

It was perfect: an idea that must have come from Practical Joke Heaven.

There were four of us who took turns unfurling the heavy roll of 24-inch plastic. We started with the front of their thirty-foot cottage, making sure to cover the door, and continued down the far side and across the back. We took turns, keeping the shrink-wrap taut. Around we went: four times, five times, and then six—which effectively sealed Ken and Donna's cottage from use.

Saturday morning arrived. There was no doubt we conspirators were smug, and beside ourselves with delight over the practical joke we had played on The King. Waiting until Ken arrived proved to be difficult.

Saturday afternoon was blistering hot. The evening came and went, offering scant reprieve from the oppressive heat. The conspirators and their spouses worried about the whereabouts of Ken and Donna. Eventually, everyone retired for the evening. There was no sign of Ken and Donna.

Sunday morning came, followed by another blistering hot afternoon. Still, there was no sign of Ken and Donna. We reasoned that it was a long weekend, and that our friends would arrive sometime on Monday.

Finally, just before noon on Monday, the waylaid couple arrived. They were no doubt hot, tired, and delighted to finally be at the lake. We assumed they couldn't wait to get into shorts and out into their boat.

The conspirators kept out of sight, waiting for audible signs that the practical joke had hit a bull's-eye. Nothing. An hour later, we still hadn't heard anything.

Finally, the suspense became too much for us. We decided to sneak over to Ken and Donna's as a group. We were shocked by what we saw.

The couple was there and they were busy. Ken was packing garbage bags full of something into the back of his truck. He was not in a pleasant frame of mind. Donna appeared from the cottage with another full garbage bag. She looked even more unhappy than Ken.

The truth emerged. Our fiendish practical joke had backfired in a very big way. With amazing restraint, Ken and Donna informed "the conspirators" that the shrink wrap had blocked the fridge vent that protruded from the back of the cottage. Heat had built up, tripping the circuit breaker, and the freezer had shut down. Several dozen pounds of frozen meat had turned rancid in the hot midsummer weather. An assortment of other foods had also spoiled.

Oops.

We all slunk away—humbled and deeply embarrassed. Our spouses scolded us too, just to make sure we got the message.

Of course, we offered to replace the lost food, but Ken and Donna would have none of it. So the four of us decided to leave peace offerings. Over the next few days, they were placed on Ken and Donna's deck in the form of their favorite wines, beer, and rum.

But not long after each peace offering was furnished, it somehow ended up back on the deck of the conspirator who'd made the offering. That is, the beer made its way back to the beer donor's deck, the bottles of wine to the wine donor, and the rum to the person who had gifted the rum.

Nothing more was said about the day we shrink-wrapped Ken's cottage. But make no mistake: Ken got the last laugh. He always did.

Happily, the practical jokes haven't stopped. Perish the thought!

James Osborne is the author of two novels and more than seventy short stories, many of them set in cottage country. His award-winning stories have been published in regional, national and international anthologies. While he's lived in cities out of necessity for most of his career, Osborne's heart remains in the country. Read more of Osborne's stories at www.jamesosbornenovels.com.

Moose and Mosquitoes

Family vacations are easy … said nobody ever.

By Kaitlin Roland

"Daaaaaaad … are we there yet?"

Ten-year-old Viola kicked her legs into the back of the driver's seat, stretching them as far as they would go. Her father John, with a slightly maniacal look in his eye, responded without turning his head.

"Yes, Vi. Almost there. Can you STOP doing that?" He spoke through gritted teeth.

Viola sighed heavily and turned her attention to her little brother Rupert, who was sleeping next to her, his head lolling with the motion of the vehicle. She began shredding little pieces of tissue, balling them up and trying to land one in his open mouth.

The family had been on the road for three days in a rented silver minivan. It was supposed to be an epic cross-country adventure—the kids' first time across Canada—and no mountain trail would be too steep, no back road too remote. John wanted his children to experience the *true* Canadian outdoors as he had with his own father long ago.

The five of them—John, his wife Georgia, his father John Sr. (Grandpa), Viola, and Rupert—had been in the van for over nine hours that day. Tempers were short, and Georgia had taken to ignoring all fights between siblings and/or grandparent. Her eyes were glazed from lack of sleep as she balanced a paperback between her fingers.

For a few short minutes there was silence in the van. Finally, John saw the turn off for the Jasper Moose Inn, a property with a collection of rustic cottages nestled in the woods. The Inn had been around forever, and Grandpa had insisted on spending at least one night at this "fine example of hospitality." John signaled and made the turn just as a rogue tissue ball landed in his ear. He was glad they had arrived.

At the front desk, Georgia checked the family in while the rest of the family milled about. The man behind the counter, who was wearing a red flannel shirt unbuttoned to the chest, chatted amicably about the weather. On a map, he showed Georgia where their cottage—which he'd chosen for optimal privacy and a "true experience of nature"—was located. Grandpa watched over Georgia's shoulder, chuckling good-naturedly. "Excellent! Kids, you're going to get the real outdoor experience!"

"It looks wonderful," agreed Georgia. "Everyone back in the van. And Rupert—put that stick down." She narrowed her eyes at Rupert, who reluctantly lowered the stick and moved it away from his sister's ankles. It was clearly bedtime.

The family marched back toward the silver beast and climbed inside. They drove down the gravel lane in darkness, Georgia attempting to navigate with the map while Grandpa shone a flashlight on it. John sat in the back sear and sang Disney songs with the kids.

Finally, they pulled up to the cottage. In the van's headlights she could see that the building was short and squat, and had white paint peeling from its exterior. It also had a rickety porch that only looked wide enough for two people.

She heard gasps from the kids. "We're supposed to sleep there?" they said in unison. "Mom, isn't this like where they shoot horror movies?"

Their haunted reverie was interrupted by grumblings from Grandpa, who was already taking his bags out of the van and walking toward the front door.

John and Georgia piled the kids high with bags (if only to stifle their voices) and marched them inside. A lumpy old couch, a tiny kitchenette, and two bedrooms greeted them—each with one double bed.

"Now this is living!" exclaimed Grandpa. He cracked open a beer he had taken from some unknown stash. "I used to come here in the fall to fish and hunt, and boy, it was wonderful. Your dad and I used to stay in a cabin just like this!"

Rupert and Viola looked around, less than impressed. As they fiddled with the TV, intrigued by the fact that turning knobs was necessary to change the channel, John and Georgia quickly unpacked a few necessary items.

"It's only one night," he quietly reminded her. "Dad loves it here. Rupert and I will take him fishing in the morning while you and Vi sleep in. After that, we'll stand a better chance of surviving the long drive tomorrow."

Georgia gave a noncommittal grunt. After fifteen years with John and his father, she doubted that it would be that simple.

Within a half hour, everyone had brushed their teeth and climbed into bed. The cabin was stifling inside, which meant everyone had stripped down to their underwear. Georgia and Viola shared one bed, Rupert and his grandpa the other, while John camped out on the couch. The cottage settled and soon the sounds of sleep—both light breathing and heavy snoring—could be heard coming from the various rooms.

Not twenty minutes later, Viola whispered, "Mom, do you hear that?"

"Viola, I do hear it. It's a mosquito. Just ignore it and go back to sleep."

"But mom, I-I-I hear it close by. Like I think it's by my ear."

"OK, pull the covers over your head, then."

"But mom, it's really hot. Oh no! There it is again!"

"Viola, I am exhausted. Your father is exhausted. And you are also probably exhausted. Just count sheep in your head and you'll forget about the mosquito."

Viola went quiet and tried to follow her mother's instructions. Silence returned and Georgia began to drift off to sleep again.

"Grandpa. GRANDPA! I think I've got him!" Georgia could hear Rupert's voice screeching through the wall. It sounded like somebody was jumping on the bed in the room next door, each bounce followed by a loud slapping sound.

"Get 'em, Rupert! GET 'EM!" Grandpa was shouting encouragement.

"What in the blazes is going on in there?" Georgia said, throwing off her sheets and heading into the front room. Viola followed close behind, concerned that the lone mosquito might return in her mother's absence.

Georgia opened the door to the next room and poked her head around the doorframe. "For goodness' sake, John, what are you DOING?"

Grandpa was still lying in bed, the covers pulled up to his chin. Rupert was perched in the corner, a focused grin on his face. John was standing on the bed, wearing only his briefs, with a small white washcloth held tight in his hand. He was whipping it outwards, slapping it against the walls.

"Stand back, Georgie!" he shouted, half-laughing. "We're under attack!"

"What in the…" She reached for the light switch.

"No, mom, don't do that…" Rupert squealed.

Before he was able to finish, she had turned on the lights. As soon as she did, she could see that the room was filled with mosquitoes, swarming all over the room. The walls were covered with tiny specks of red—casualties of John's towel attack.

"Must've been a bloody nest under the cottage!" bellowed Grandpa, who was clearly enjoying himself. "Never seen anything like this!"

John leapt off the bed and handed the towel to Rupert. "Keep at it, son. I've got to check the rest of the cottage." And like a man at war, he sprinted into the front room, turning on all the lights as he went. "Good Lord, they're coming through the floorboards!"

This was too much for Viola, who began to clutch her mother's arm anxiously. "Mom. MOM! All I can hear is buzzing. It's like in my head! There are so many, I can't take it. What if I get bit a million times and die?"

Georgia looked at her daughter with wide eyes. Her son was now jumping up and down on the bed while Grandpa cheered him on: "Get those buggers!"

Then she heard her husband exclaim from the bathroom, "Wow! They've made it through the tiles too!"

Georgia closed her eyes for a moment. "OK. That's enough, everyone. Rupert: put on your pajama shirt. Viola: go find a sweater. It's late and we have a lot of driving tomorrow, which means Vi and Rupert are coming with me. We're sleeping in the van."

She looked at her husband, daring him to disagree. It was well past midnight and they still had a twelve-hour drive ahead of them the following day.

Her husband smiled innocently. "Sure, no problem. Here are the keys." He threw them to Georgia, and without another glance he headed back into the bedroom to speak with Grandpa about possible mosquito annihilation tactics.

Georgia grabbed pillows for herself and each child and headed out toward the van. The night had cooled down and the ground felt dewy beneath their bare feet. She set Viola up at the very back, which would allow her to lie down comfortably. She put Rupert in one of the middle seats, and then took the passenger seat for herself and locked the van. As the lights dimmed and everyone settled in, she started to relax. Maybe they would end up getting a good rest after all.

"Mom?" Rupert's voice cut through the silence like a knife.

Georgia opened one eye. "Mm hmm?"

"Mom, I think there's a moth in here. I saw it when we got in and I know it's still here. I can feel it *looking* at me."

Viola, hearing this, curled into a ball in the back seat. She whimpered, "Mom, I hate moths! I hate them more than mosquitoes!"

Georgia turned in her seat and looked at her children. They later recounted that the look on her face was similar to what a jaguar must look like before it attacks. Rupert even claimed that her head swiveled all the way around.

Georgia took a deep breath through her nose, collecting herself. "Well, if there is a moth, he's surely dead by now."

"But mom, what if he isn't?"

"I'm not wrong Rupert. He is. I promise you."

"But moooooom…"

"THE MOTH IS DEAD! Now GO to sleep!"

She doubted the children were convinced, but for some reason, they did as they were told. Soon their quick, anxious breathing became slow and steady, and she could tell that they had fallen asleep.

"Next time, it's my turn to pick a hotel," said Georgia quietly to herself.

She balanced her head on the seatbelt, closed her eyes, and tried to pretend that she was not in the front seat of a van. Outside, the sounds of the crickets offered a strange counterpoint to the slapping and hoots of laughter still coming from inside the cottage.

*A poor excuse for a Girl Guide, Kaitlin Roland spent many summers in the wilds of northwestern Ontario, hoping her father wouldn't lose her on one of his nature "walks." He didn't. She now writes for a living, splitting her time between the world of advertising and attempts to make her cat a YouTube sensation. You can visit her online at **www.kateroland.com**.*

My Space

Let's hope they never invent the iCottage.

By Pamela Patchet

Twitter was the straw that broke this techno-overloaded camel's back. I had already listened to the multitudes of fans who convinced me to join Facebook, MySpace, LinkedIn, and Blogger. I have several email accounts and I've joined forums and Listservs—the cyber equivalent of hanging around the water cooler to discuss work or the latest reality show. I have an iPod and an iPhone, but increasingly less "I" time. We have more laptops in our house than pets. And we have a lot of pets.

My cell phone ensures people can reach me anywhere, anytime—and they *do!* And now I'm told even that isn't enough. I've got to "tweet" to stay in the loop, even though that loop is threatening to turn into a noose. Twitter, if you haven't already heard, is an online platform that limits communication to a sentence or two. Once you've signed up for an account, you can follow friends or celebrities who "tweet" things like "I am buying cute shoes!" or "I had a dream I could fly using turnips as wings!"

Do I really need this?

Help! I think I might have Online Sociability Fatigue, and I can't get up. The cure? Take two weeks at the cottage and *don't* call me in the morning.

At the lake we have spotty dial-up access to the Internet and no cell service, cable, or satellite signal. Truly desperate guests can watch *Ghostbusters* on a VCR connected to a battered twelve-inch television set. Or they can read a book the old-fashioned way—you know, by actually holding a book and flipping pages.

Time at the cottage calls to mind the kind of old-fashioned summers that I had as a kid: building tree forts with scavenged lumber, playing impromptu baseball games, or skating with roller skates clamped onto sneakers and tightened with a key. All we needed was a skipping rope, or an elastic cord for "jumpsies," or a rubber ball. BYOB meant "Bring your own blue velvet Crown Royal bag full of marbles." We had unfettered freedom to get dirty and to figure out the best way to stay occupied during the day.

At the cottage, an old log bench under a pine tree becomes our living room, and the nightly bonfire under a starry sky our big-screen TV. Without the constant need to be plugged in with our electronic toys, we all calm down and revert to our most basic selves. If you want entertainment, you create it: build a sand castle, catch and release frogs, roast potatoes in the embers, recite stories, sing songs.

I could buy a satellite dish for our cottage. But why would I? I love that my mind sinks into the same stillness that I feel when I lower myself onto our big down-filled sofa with a fat novel. It's only in this stillness that I begin to really think, to let go, and to let the stress of everyday life dissolve. It's probably more accurate to say that I become my true self again. Even physical work, like stacking wood, digging holes for a new cedar fence, or weeding—they all become tasks that build the body while freeing the mind.

Dinner parties at the cottage are casual affairs that usually entail a good group of friends gathering on our deck to eat barbecued burgers, fresh corn on the cob dripping with butter and salt, and garden-fresh tomatoes warm from the vine with a sprinkle of olive oil and basil. Add to this scene a dog underfoot and a cold beer in hand, whispered secrets under the stars, the warm embrace of a loved one as we dance outside to tunes we listened to in high school. What more do we really need?

When I want to write, I don't plug in my laptop—I pull out a pad of paper and a pen.

When I want to cool off, I don't turn on an air conditioner—I jump in the lake.

When I want to exercise, I don't head off to the fitness club or jump on a treadmill—I grab the dog and trundle off down our dirt road, adding an extra hour or two for the neighbors I'll meet along the way who will want to discuss the latest council move or tax change or grandchild or big catch.

When I want to watch television, I head for the dock at sunset, where the greatest show on earth is spread out before me. It's a show that is original every night—it never goes into reruns. If I'm truly blessed, I'll be rewarded with pulsating sheets of the aurora borealis reflected in the dark waters.

Instead of picking up the phone, I'll call out over the fence or shout to a passing canoe. "Hey, how's it going, eh?" For you never sound more Canadian than when you're shouting to someone in a canoe.

"Not bad, not bad," they'll answer. "You?"

"Pretty good," I'll say. "Can't complain."

And it is. And I can't.

I think the only twittering I'll be keeping track of this summer will come from the chickadees eating out of my outstretched palm on a quiet summer's morning, with a gentle breeze lifting my hair from my face and the warm sun on my back.

Pamela Patchet is a former ad executive turned freelance writer. She observes the human experience, then tries to make sense of it, preferably on her cottage dock with a cocktail in hand. Her work has appeared in several anthologies, The Globe and Mail, The National Post, *and* The Montreal Gazette, *and she has a regular column in* Watershed Magazine. *Visit her at* **www.anovelwoman.blogspot.com**.

The Lost Boys

Boys will be boys will be boys...

By Greg Simison

The fact that, regardless of age, boys will be boys was brought home to me a few years ago when my brother and I spent three days with our sons at his cottage. This cottage is located on a pine-covered island in the Rideau Lakes system south of Ottawa. Nothing brings the boy out in a man faster than living the childhood fantasy of having one's home on an island. If you scratch the skin of any middle-aged man, it's quite likely that Peter Pan or Robinson Crusoe will emerge.

It was during a conversation on our last day that an idea was triggered in both my brother and his son. Their faces simultaneously broke into the same evil grin. After ordering us to stay put, they disappeared around the side of the cottage and into the dark storage area located beneath the building. For the next thirty minutes we heard nothing but the clanking of tools mixed with frequent giggles. When we were finally called, little did we know that it would be a call to arms.

Arriving at the dock, we saw what appeared to be an erected telescope. Closer inspection revealed something much more sinister.

"What is that?" I asked.

Through his Alfred E. Newman grin, my brother said, "It's a potato cannon."

"Well, of course it is," I responded, wondering if his thirty years working as a civil servant had finally caught up with him. My son gave me a frightened look, at what appeared to be the first substantial evidence of insanity on my side of the family. It had long ago been recognized as rampant on his mother's side.

My brother explained that the construction of this weapon had been a "bonding project" they'd worked on the previous winter after coming across the plans in an old 1950s copy of *Popular Mechanics*. The fact that he's probably exchanged fewer than a dozen words with his son since then reinforces my belief that bonding only works if it involves large amounts of Super Glue. In any case, I won't go into the details on how this weapon works, since some bright kid is sure to read this and end up with a potato permanently lodged in one of his nostrils. (I'd be happy to provide blueprints to any of you out there whose children, like mine, deserve such a fate.)

After a long lecture on safety procedures, we each fired the gun and watched potatoes soar several hundred feet out onto the lake. It was wonderful. Peter would have killed for such a weapon, for he could have taken care of both Captain Hook and the crocodile once and for all. I mean, where else can you find a weapon—other than a pea shooter—that fires biodegradable ammunition and at the same time provides a loud and satisfying *bang* that all children long for?

Within minutes the boys had lost interest. They wandered off while my brother and I, losing all restraint, spent the afternoon working our way through a fifty-pound bag of Prince Edward Island's finest.

It was as the sun fled west, in order to get out of range, that we realized we needed a greater challenge. And, further evidence that God is a boy at heart, it was at this point that two canoeists dared to try and paddle through our firing zone. It's amazing the speed that a fiberglass canoe can attain when powered by four arms and sheer terror. Their screams, unfortunately, attracted the attention of our thirteen-year-old sons.

There's nothing more depressing, or fun-killing, than children who possess a sense of responsibility. We were sternly lectured, and even threatened with the confiscation of the cannon, if we continued to display such childish behavior. "Under no circumstance should you fire at living things," we were told. We contritely hung our heads and promised (with fingers crossed behind our backs) that we would behave.

An awkward silence fell over the island. But it was short-lived.

It was then that we heard in the distance an unmistakable high-pitched whine that rapidly grew into a familiar scream that is capable of bonding fathers and sons—and indeed *all* true cottagers—in a common cause.

"Load the potato gun," my son ordered through gritted teeth.

"Top up that fuel chamber!" his cousin shouted.

My brother and I jumped to obey. The sights were adjusted. The fuel added. The hardest potato we could find was jammed down the barrel. A coin was tossed to see who would get to fire the fatal shot.

The Sea-Doo rounded the point and flew across the bay, moving tantalizingly close to the firing zone.

"Justifiable homicide," my son muttered as he wiped the sweat from his brow.

Greg Simison lives in Moose Jaw, Saskatchewan. His fifth book, Miscellaneous Wreckage, *was released by Thistledown Press in the fall of 2014. The cannon described in The Lost Boys is currently being dismantled prior to being donated to the PEI Potato Hall of Fame.*

Moby Dick

The one that (thankfully) got away.

By Jeff Groberman

My father and I had an annual ritual. Every year from the time I was eight he would take me to Horseshoe Bay near Vancouver, where we'd rent a boat at Sewell's Marina and drag a herring around the ocean for several hours. We'd inevitably finish the ritual with a bowl of clam chowder at Troll's, a restaurant known for its English-style fish and chips.

We never caught a thing.

In my mid twenties—after fifteen years of not catching a single fish—I decided we should go on a father-son fishing trip where we *actually* stood a chance of catching something. I arranged for a trip to Campbell River, a picturesque town on Vancouver Island that's known for its seaside cottages with views across Discovery Passage to Quadra Island. Once there, we would charter a boat and a guide.

I knew things were off to a rocky start when we met our guide and boat. The boat was a twelve-foot open-air Lund, and our guide was only thirteen years old. During the two days we were in Campbell River, my father caught a crab, a bird, a rock, and a couple of bottom fish; I caught nothing.

On our last day, we were fishing just off the mouth of the river. My father, being a non-swimmer, likes to stay close to land

and away from large ferries, of which he has a pathological fear. Moments before it was time to pack up and leave, a fish hit my line. I could tell by the way the line leapt off the reel that the fish was a big one. In fact, I could feel the *thrum thrum thrum* of the fish's tail beating through the water.

After playing the fish for about twenty minutes, I noticed that my father was staring off into the distance. His lips were moving, but no sound was coming out. I turned to the guide and he too was speechless. I shifted to see what they were looking at: it appeared to be a large saw blade cutting through the water right for our boat.

"Killer whale!" shouted the guide.

The whale was swimming directly at our small boat, and only at the last minute did it roll over and disappear underneath. It was like watching a bus drive beneath us. The whale and my fish met about twenty feet from our boat, and the line literally began to smoke off the reel.

"You've got the whale!" my dad shouted. "Throw the rod overboard!"

My dad was now beyond reason. "Throw the rod overboard! I'll buy you a new one! I'll buy you two! Just throw the damn thing overboard!"

"I've waited twenty-two years for this fish," I replied calmly. "The damn whale can catch his own fish."

At that point the situation became moot. My line went slack as the whale surfaced about ten meters away. I reeled like mad and was rewarded with a giant fish head. Evidently the whale was in a compromising mood and had decided to split the fish with me.

He had severed the head just below the gills, and had done it so skillfully that the fish didn't even know that two-thirds of its body was missing. The gills were still moving as if nothing was wrong.

The guide netted the fish head and we sat there staring in disbelief at both the whale and my decapitated prize.

"Throw the head back," my father pleaded.

"What?"

"The whale knows you have the head. It wants it." Obviously my dad had lost touch with reality.

"No," I said. "I'm keeping the head. It's the only proof we've got that I caught a fish."

My father reluctantly agreed, as long as we went back to shore. When we landed at the marina they weighed the fish head— it weighed in at a little over fifteen pounds. They figured the whole fish would have clocked in at fifty or sixty pounds.

My father didn't stick around for the weigh-in. He went straight to the bar at the Discovery Inn and ordered a double scotch. My father hardly ever drank and never more than a sip, so ordering a double was not in character for him. All the way home he kept a wary eye trained off the stern of the ferry—just in case the whale was still looking for his missing fish head.

A lot of people have refused to believe the story, suggesting instead that a seal must have taken my fish. However, a few years later, the head of the Vancouver aquarium was a guest on the Vancouver Show (which I was producing at the time) and saw the picture of the fish head that was proudly displayed on my desk.

"Killer whale," stated Dr. Newman without hearing the story.

"How can you tell?" I asked.

"Two rows of teeth marks," he said. "Can I get a copy of that picture?"

So somewhere in the offices of the Vancouver aquarium is a picture of my encounter with a killer whale. As for my dad, he preferred to go back to dragging a herring around Horseshoe Bay, where the most dangerous thing he'd have to face were the cooked clams in the clam chowder at Troll's.

Jeff Groberman is probably best known as one of the originators of the infamous CBC seventies radio series "Dr. Bundolo's Pandemonium Medicine Show." In the eighties he became a producer on the "Vancouver Show" at CKVU, where he still hasn't lived down refusing to let John Lennon on the show. He now writes screenplays that nobody reads and travels to weird, wonderful, and dangerous places around the world. He lives in Surrey, BC.

Cape Tormentine

Surviving one's youth at a cottage on Northumberland Strait.

By Bob Dixon

Cape Tormentine is a small fishing village nestled in the southeast corner of New Brunswick. It was home to one of the ferries that used to transport trains and cars from the mainland to Borden, Prince Edward Island before the Canadian government sponsored the construction of the Confederation Bridge.

From as far back as I can remember, my parents owned a waterfront cottage at Cape Tormentine. Ours was one of eleven or twelve cottages that lined the shoreline between the Cape Tormentine ferry dock and the lighthouse at Cape Jourimain, which also sits on the New Brunswick side about four kilometers northwest of the dock. On a clear day we could see the green hills of PEI rising up over the water some fourteen kilometers away.

The cottage was where our family whiled away the summer months. For a time during my youth, we were lucky enough to own three sloops, two outboard motorboats, and a dinghy, which my father moored behind a breakwater that he had built during the 1950s. We often went motorboating or sailing on the Northumberland Strait, sometimes travelling as far as Shediac, a coastal town seventy-two kilometers to the northwest, and quite often to Prince Edward Island. We were never afraid of sailing dangerously close to an approaching ferry because we knew that sailboats had the right of way, and on more than one occasion we forced the old Abegweit ferry off course.

I was always up to something with my friends from the nearby cottages. One day, when we were all in our mid-teens, four of us got together and decided to undertake a rather adventurous plan. We were all pretty good water-skiers, so we figured we would try water-skiing thirty kilometers across Northumberland Strait to Summerside. We packed a lunch, put on life jackets, and gassed up the boat. Jim wanted to drive, so Mac was the designated lookout for the narrow passage leading to the Summerside wharf. Hal and I were on water skis. Jim aimed the boat to where we thought Summerside should be, and we took off at full speed without permission from my parents because I knew they would say no.

The trip went fine for the first while, but about two thirds of the way across, I looked to my left and saw that Hal wasn't there anymore. He had fallen and no one had noticed.

We had made no plans for those in the boat to keep a watch on the skiers. Since the two in the boat were looking ahead, I began to shake the bar in my hands to make the towline oscillate, hoping that the reverberations of the rope would attract their attention. This went on for several minutes until Mac turned around and noticed immediately that Hal was missing. By that time we were so far away from the scene of the mishap that he was completely out of sight.

Now, in addition to lots of jellyfish, the Northumberland Straight has a fairly powerful tidal current, which means that when someone falls into the water they are soon far from the place where they fell. In our case, we didn't even know where Hal had fallen, or for that matter, in what direction the tidal current was flowing.

Jim swung the boat around and headed back in the general direction from which we had come. Luck was with us: about fifteen minutes later, we saw a worried Hal bobbing in the water. Jim turned again to bring the bar on the end of the rope as close to Hal as he could. Hal swam to the bar, we resumed the proper position, and we were soon on our way to the Summerside wharf again.

Upon our return to Cape Tormentine, Jim announced that we had run out of gas just as we hit the sandbar. Then it dawned on me: I had forgotten to calculate the amount of gas we would need to get to Summerside and back!

It wasn't long after that my older brother and his girlfriend, along with me and my brother's friend Todd, decided to play nighttime hide-and-seek on the water in front of our cottage. We pulled out from behind the breakwater in our boats, armed with nothing more than flashlights and lanterns. One person was to drive off, stop the boat in a place unknown, then turn off the engine and the lights. When the boat that was seeking approached the hidden boat, the person in the hidden boat was to turn on his lights to indicate that the seeker was getting too close. It was decided that Todd and I would be the first to go and hide.

After we had stopped and turned off our lights, my brother and his girlfriend began searching for us. He accelerated his boat up to maximum speed and we watched him circle around fruitlessly for several minutes. Todd and I were sitting at opposite ends of the boat when, to our surprise, my brother turned in the dark and headed directly for us, aiming dead center at our starboard side.

As he approached, I turned on my lantern on to warn him of the impending crash. Unfortunately, the head of the lantern was on a swivel, and distracted by the oncoming boat, I didn't notice that the swivel was aiming the light directly at the floorboards. My brother couldn't see a thing.

As the bow of his speedboat rammed the side of ours, the force of impact lifted his boat out of the water. I watched with dismay as the dark form of his boat flew through the air between Todd and me—a mere foot from my face—and splashed into the water on the other side. I can still see the dark outline of the outboard motor as it passed in front of my eyes.

Miraculously, there were no injuries and no damage to his boat. Mine sustained some damage to the starboard side, but I was able to make it back to the dock.

When we got back to the cottage to inform our father of the incident, we expected to be severely reprimanded. It seemed quite strange to me that he wasn't angry, and that he actually seemed quite jovial about the entire affair. I understood why when the next day we had a boat-burning party and Dad collected on the insurance.

Today, the breakwater is virtually washed away. My older brother has just turned seventy, and my cottage friends and I are now in our sixties. Often we reminisce about these and other stories, like the day two friends and I were sailing a small sloop.

We had been swamped in shallow water over a sandbar by a gust of wind, but we were a half-mile from shore. When I dropped anchor to stabilize the boat, I discovered that the other end of the rope was not attached to the boat. The water between us and the shore was too deep to walk the boat in, so we had to wait for two hours, standing and holding the boat in four feet of water, until someone noticed that we were in difficulty and came to our rescue. If you happen to be walking along the sand flats at low tide, not far from the Cape Jourimain lighthouse, you might still come across our rusty old anchor.

The Dixon family cottage was built in the late 1940s and is now owned by the son-in-law of Bob's oldest brother. He and his wife rent it out as a luxury summer vacation home. The breakwater has since washed away so there are no more boats. This story first appeared in the Summit Studios anthology Never Trust a Smiling Bear *(2010). Bob Dixon passed away in 2012.*

Faith in the Redwoods

The kind of place where you find cats, bongo drums, and information about top secret FBI plots.

By Laurie Gough

After years of searching I may have finally found the perfect place to live, although I haven't moved in yet so I can't be entirely sure. An hour and a half north of San Francisco, in Sonoma County, is a town called Camp Meeker. I've decided to rent a room in a rustic home entirely surrounded by redwoods. My bed will be in a glass-encased loft, and all around me will be thousand-year-old giants. Faith Fauna is the name of the woman who owns the cottage, although I'm sure that can't be her real name. I saw her ad on a bulletin board in Occidental:

> **LOOKING FOR VEGAN HOUSEMATE TO SHARE LOVELY
> HOUSE IN TREES. NON-SMOKER, MUST
> LOVE ANIMALS, NO PETS (SINCE I HAVE CATS).
> $350/MONTH.**

The ad also had a map showing where the house is located and a phone number for a health food store in Santa Rosa where Faith Fauna works. Faith Fauna sounded very cheerful on the phone and she thought I did, too. When she asked if I was vegan, I told her honestly that I eat cheese sometimes but had been planning to cut it out. Also, I admitted to having a weakness for ice cream, although it usually makes me feel terrible afterwards, so I agreed to cut that out, too.

I drove a mile down the winding Bohemian Highway from Occidental until I came to an old wooden sign that stretched above the road. It read: CAMP MEEKER. I had trouble getting my car up the steep and narrow roads into Camp Meeker, but I arrived early, so I parked and spent some time walking around the place.

Camp Meeker is a cluster of about three hundred homes hidden beneath a dark forest canopy where narrow roads rollercoaster through it like an accident waiting to happen. The place isn't big enough to have its own general store, but there's a post office that sits in a trailer beneath the trees. Most of the homes are small and appear even smaller because they're dwarfed by three-hundred-foot redwoods. The homes are all made of wood and look as though gnomes live in them.

When it was time to meet Faith Fauna, I walked up about fifty steps to get to her home. Once inside, I knew immediately that it was where I wanted to live. Luckily, she felt I belonged there too and said that I could move in immediately.

*   *   *

When I arrived at Faith Fauna's cottage, she was waiting to help me unpack. Not that I had much with me. In fact, our project for the day was to buy a futon mattress for my room and a used couch for her living room. In Santa Rosa, we also visited the health food store where she's a manager, and she introduced me to her friends. They're all vibrant student-types—brimming with enthusiasm, wheatgrass juice, and detailed plans to change the world.

That evening, Faith told me she was going to cook a specialty of hers. Most vegan food is delicious and I wondered what she would make. Turns out that her specialty is whole-wheat pasta with beet sauce. "This will transport you to another place," she told me. I took a bite and sure enough, it did: a Siberian labor camp. However, the vegan brownies we had for dessert were scrumptious.

As Faith poured some blueberry tea, she told me about growing up in Florida, how she used to follow the Grateful Dead across the continent in a van, and how she was able to buy the cottage when her father left money for her after he'd gone to jail in the Savings and Loan crisis. We continued chatting after dinner, relaxing on the new couch in the living room—a cozy sunken room with circular windows, bongo drums along the wall, hanging ferns, and several bent-willow chairs that were interesting to look at but nothing you'd ever want to sit in. We shared bad date stories and laughed about how hard it was for women in their thirties to find the perfect guy. I liked Faith Fauna.

I went to bed feeling thrilled with my new surroundings, and sank luxuriously into my new cushy futon inside the glass-enclosed loft. Rain fell gently all night long, pattering through the leaves just outside my open window. I inhaled the misty cool air, taking deep breaths of California. I felt a familiar, wild happiness.

After several days, I've started to learn a lot about Faith Fauna. She is an animal rights activist, a strict vegan, and an Earth First! member. She hosts secret meetings in her home that she thinks are monitored by the FBI. She owns six cats, most of them vicious bird killers, which seems to run counter to her animal rights stance since every day one of the felines deposits a dead bird on her kitchen floor. Since she's a vegan, she doesn't want any animal products in her home—with the exception of dead birds. I'm not allowed to bring ice cream into the cottage, or butter, or even my old suede jacket. I don't mind too much. I'm feeling very healthy.

Faith Fauna has many interesting friends: Egrett, who likes to come by on the full moon; Saffron, who looks like one of Charlie's Angels; Feral, who lives in a teepee; Cool Mama; a guy named Jenny; Sha-na-na; and Anarchy. Anarchy lives inside redwood trees to keep them from being chopped down. She needs a bath. Anarchy stinks.

One night, I burned one of Faith Fauna's cats. I've never been a cat lover—the hair, the dander, the bird killing, the litter, the unspoken demands, the attitude. But I certainly didn't mean to harm this cat. The cat was on top of the stove when I wanted to turn on an element. Faith Fauna lets her cats go wherever they please. The cat was bugging me up there, and giving me some attitude. So I turned the gas stove to high, thinking that I was turning on the front element when it actually was the back one. I only wanted to startle the cat. When the back burner flared up, a yellow flame immediately transferred to the cat and a good chunk of its fur caught on fire for a few seconds. The curious thing was, the cat didn't care. It just stood up, stretched, and jumped off the stove. Ten minutes later I was watching a movie and the cat was curled up on my lap. I noticed a substantial patch of missing hair along its side.

*   *   *

Two days later, Faith Fauna brought me along to one of her political protests with some of her friends, a highly-susceptible-to-conspiracy-theories bunch with good hearts and disheveled bird-nesty hair. We were demonstrating against biogenetic engineering by performing street theater in front of Safeway. Some of the group dressed as giant tomatoes and ran away from a mad scientist who was waving around a bovine growth hormone injection. Other people dressed as pigs with fish fins coming out of their heads, or vegetables with animal noses. My job was to video all of this, which meant that I got to enjoy myself without dressing as a mutant turnip. When some of Faith's friends ran into the store to attach stickers on baby food saying, GMO CONTAMINATED!, the manager chased them back outside. We made the local news.

Later that night I was in my bedroom writing when I heard a knock at the door. Faith wasn't home, so I got up to answer it. Even before I got there, I could hear a high-pitched voice that was fraught with tension saying, "Anyone home? Anyone home?" When I opened the door, a woman who looked to be in her mid-forties was stroking one of Faith Fauna's cats. She had black-and-white frizzy hair that cascaded down her back like a wild mane. I invited her inside.

When we sat down in the kitchen, she asked me what kind of tea we had. "Well, let's see," I said. "There seems to be all the regular herbal ones, and some Chinese varieties." Thinking she might need something to calm her nerves, I suggested chamomile.

"I want to try to get pregnant, but not until January," she suddenly blurted.

I looked at her, this woman whose adolescence seemed to have congealed beneath the wrinkles of middle age. Then I looked down at the boxes of tea in my hands. "Do you need a special tea for that? For fertility or something?"

"Yeah, probably, but I told you I don't want to get pregnant until January. If I wait till January to get pregnant, then I'll give birth to a Virgo Rabbit. I want a Rabbit to get along with a Pig. I'm a Pig and so is my son. Chinese astrology."

"Oh, right."

"I definitely don't want to give birth to a Rooster. I hate Roosters. My ex-husband is a Rooster. Roosters are assholes."

"Oh, so who do you want to have the baby with?"

"My ex-husband."

"The Rooster?"

"Yeah," she said, as if it were obvious.

I stared at her hair. It looked like an unruly multidirectional headdress. "So why are you telling me this?"

"I tell everybody this." She spoke in a tone that suggested ongoing bitterness, a tone that discouraged me from asking further questions.

I boiled water for the tea while she sat down with a cat on a beanbag chair in the corner. Luckily, just then, Faith returned home with a fellow named Earle, who works with her at the health food store. Earle is a poet. While we sat drinking green tea and eating hemp carob muffins, Earle, Faith, and the Chinese astrology woman got into a conversation about how the FBI introduced crack cocaine and guns into the ghettos of New York City to get rid of all the non-whites. It seemed a little far-fetched to me, but under the circumstances, all I could do was go with the flow. After a while, I managed to escape back to my room.

OK, so it's a little flakey here, but it can be flakey anywhere. Just two years ago in my hometown of Guelph, Ontario, I lived with three friends in an old Victorian house. The vegetarian landlady who lived beneath us came upstairs once a week, ostensibly to vacuum, but really to sift through our trash for frozen chicken wrappers or old torn-up recipes—any evidence that we had eaten meat. She wanted a vegetarian household since she claimed dead animal flesh upset the energy balance of the house, disturbed her dreams, and stunk up the kitchen. We never did eat meat while living there, but she didn't believe us. She insisted that she often felt a vibe of carnage seeping down through the ceiling. Her husband, an anemic-looking waif of a man who hardly spoke, had placed copies of the appallingly written *Celestine Prophecy* on each of our beds when we moved in. He explained that it was required reading for anyone who lived there. Our beds, incidentally, all had to be facing north—something to do with the magnetic pull of the earth.

No. California doesn't have a monopoly on flakiness. And besides, not everyone in the state is like these people. It's only one of many California communities. I just had to try harder to make new friends—with people I could relate to.

*   *   *

It was this realization that led me to a dinner party in Sebastopol, held at the home of a botanist named Gerry Green. (Seriously, does everyone invent a name around here?) As each guest arrived, Gerry taped a piece of paper with both common name and Latin name of a plant to our foreheads. We then had to guess the name of our plant by mingling with other guests and asking questions like, "Do I flower?" or "Am I deciduous?"

I kept asking, "Can you smoke me?" which most people only laughed politely at, so I started asking other questions. It was actually fun in a nerdy kind of way. It turned out that "sugar maple" was taped to my forehead, which I think Gerry chose for me on purpose because he knew that I was from eastern Canada. When it finally hit me to ask, "Do I turn red?" everyone shouted in unison "Yes!" The whole experience had a strange effect on me: it made me sad for being so far away from the sugar maples. It also made me realize that if I lived here I wouldn't see them anymore.

The people at the party were all friendly, fun, and intelligent. I kept wondering if they could be my new friends. At the same time, I remembered that I already had friends back home. In making new ones, would I be replacing the old?

As I was contemplating all of this, a woman named Cheron sat down beside me and told me that she had also just moved there— from upstate New York. She was an artist who turned cutlery into sculptures and wanted to open her own studio. She was also very hygienic. She told me that if a tall man ever came to visit me, that I should ask him to sit down on the toilet to urinate rather than stand. She explained that this was because tall men always splash and have the habit of getting their pee all over the bathroom floor, which is dangerously unsanitary. She had even seen this on Oprah.

I'm not sure that I can be friends with Cheron.

I do like it at Camp Meeker, despite the fact that some of the people I've met here are—how can I say it politely—a little extreme? I've always dreamed of living by the ocean, and it's only twenty minutes away. I've also dreamed of living in a place where nature is enormous, magnificent, and lushly green. And doesn't host winter. My ideal would be to live in a remote wilderness, yet be close enough to civilization so that I can buy Ben and Jerry's chocolate peanut butter ice cream. I've found all of that in California. In many ways, it's really the perfect place.

Now if only I didn't have to sneak out to my car to eat the ice cream.

Laurie Gough is author of Kiss the Sunset Pig: An American Road Trip with Exotic Detours *(Penguin) and* Kite Strings of the Southern Cross: A Woman's Travel Odyssey. *The latter book was shortlisted for the Thomas Cook Travel Book Award in the UK, and was the silver medal winner of* ForeWord Magazine's *Travel Book of the Year in the US. Twenty of her stories have been anthologized in literary travel books, and she's a regular contributor to several national newspapers. You can visit her at* **www.lauriegough.com** *or follow her blog at* **www.travelwritinglife.com***.*

A Porcupine Ate My Cabin

*Lessons learned the hard way are still learned ... but
they can sure cost a lot of money.*

By Bruce Day

When you are young, your life experiences and world view
are simple, like the outer layer of an onion. As you mature,
you discover that the onion has many, many layers.

When I was twenty-one years old, I purchased a fifty-
acre forested property near Markdale, Ontario. I was studying
landscape architecture and horticulture because I had always
enjoyed spending time outside, beneath Ontario's diverse forest
canopy. Sugar maples and black cherries, white ash and yellow
birch, basswoods and cedars; the list is endless. Hiking and
camping were my weekend activities, pursuits my dad and friends
had always encouraged and supported when I was younger.

My friends and I enjoyed things in a very simple way when
I first started driving up there from Toronto, where I lived at the
time. We slept in tents and used an elevated horizontal log for
answering calls of nature.

We didn't realize we were not alone.

My first attempt at building something was an outhouse.
(I had begun to yearn for improvements to the facilities to prevent
bruised hips and slivers.) So I recruited some friends and family

members and we built it out of three-quarter inch plywood, with creosote painted on the bottom four feet of the walls and door. We were very proud of that outhouse for the first few weeks. The new plywood, however, must have smelled to the resident porcupines like turkey and stuffing smells to us. They had soon eaten a hole through the side; next, they began eating away at the insides of the walls.

So we installed aluminum printing sheets around the bottom of the outhouse, roughly three feet high. With this protection installed, I felt sure that my challenges were over.

A few weekends later, I arrived to find that in addition to plywood glue, a porcupine's diet includes aluminum. They had chewed another hole straight through the aluminum and the plywood, and had structurally destroyed the outhouse. The building was teetering, and when I looked inside I began to understand why. The critters had eaten through eleven-sixteenths of the twelve-sixteenths of plywood on the inside walls, as high up as they could reach. They had also devoured the entire vertical splashboard under the front of the toilet seat, along with at least ninety-five percent of the horizontal sheet that the toilet seat sat upon.

In essence, the seat was hovering above a gaping emptiness. All that was keeping it up was the five percent of wood still intact around the hinges. I guess the porcupines had somehow known when to stop eating. I'll bet you could have put a dime on the toilet seat and watched the outhouse collapse. There was nothing to save, so I destroyed it and used what little material remained to fill a low area nearby.

I was beginning to realize I was not alone.

There was a half-acre clearing on my property, and my next project was figuring out what to do with it. After much thought, I decided to fill it with some beautiful red pines. I planted two hundred in the clearing, thinking I was doing the resident deer a favor. I figured they could use the trees for shelter from the winter winds.

The new trees, however, must have smelled to the porcupines like turkey and stuffing smells to us, because those poor trees never reached twenty feet in height. They were so badly chewed and girdled by the porcupines that I had to cut them down and use them to fill low areas nearby.

I now *knew* I was not alone, but I didn't learn.

Porcupines are nocturnal, which means it was rare to see them around the property. One day, however, one of them came unexpectedly to visit while I was entertaining some friends and family. *Here's my chance*, I thought. *It's time to teach this fellow a lesson, make sure he knows he's not welcome.*

I found a large wooden box, approached slowly, then quickly dropped the box upside down over the porcupine. I set fire to some paper and dry grass inside the box to "smoke him out." A few of us banged on the outside of the crate and made lots of noise, hoping that when we let him out he would waddle away as fast as his stubby legs could take him. I figured we would never see him again.

We could hear him sneezing inside the smoky crate, so I figured he'd had enough. I turned over the crate to release him, whereupon he waddled purposefully to the first tree, climbed straight up, and then spent the next several hours defecating all over our makeshift kitchen table. What a mess!

I knew we were not alone and I was *beginning* to learn.

My sixteen-year-old Volkswagen Beetle was becoming ornery, and one winter day that year I had to leave it at my property due to mechanical problems. I caught the bus home to Toronto, and by the time I was able to return, it was late spring and my Beetle had been sitting in the snow and cold all winter long.

My "friends" had discovered my only means of transportation, and I guess the road salt on the tires must have smelled to them like turkey and stuffing smells to us, because all four tires were so badly chewed that they looked to be the thickness of one-ply toilet paper. They also ate the tire from my wheelbarrow, and the taillight covers on my sad-looking car.

I was beginning to learn, but I was learning the *hard* way.

The project for that next year was to start on a cabin. But this time, construction was going to be different. My friends, family members and I were not going to use plywood, glue, aluminum, red pine, rubber, plastic, or any of those foreign products made by man. I decided to use materials right from the local forest so that the porcupines could live in harmony with their invaders. The porcupines were there first, I realized, and I figured that if we were sensitive to their home, we could all live in harmony.

We were building a ten-sided post-and-beam building. It would have ten posts on the outside perimeter, five posts in the middle of the building, and one post in the center. I planned to have a ground floor, a second floor ten feet higher, and a loft twenty-five to thirty feet off the ground.

We worked hard that summer. We dug the holes for the maple posts and concrete footings by hand; sifted the excavated products to separate sand and stones, also by hand; and cut down maple trees with a two-man saw and peeled them. We stood the poles up in the holes with the use of a block and tackle. We hauled water by hand from a creek down the road and mixed thirty tons of concrete on sheets of plywood. It was a *huge* amount of work, but we didn't mind. We would soon get to enjoy the fruits of our labor.

When I returned the next spring, a funny thing had happened to the cabin. We had left it the fall before with two floors complete and the roof on ... but the porcupines had found it. Those critters had chewed through the ten-foot poles like beavers and brought this large structure to its knees in short order. It had collapsed and slid into a shallow valley, another low area of the property.

I was distraught, but I was also *determined* to stay and enjoy this beautiful wooded property. Porcupines or not.

So my very patient friends and I built a small cabin with a sheet metal skirting around the bottom. I encouraged the guys to "mark their territory" on nearby trees. This strategy worked, and I haven't had problems for years.

I now get along just fine with the porcupines.

I have learned a lot about these animals that roam the woods at night, and I believe strongly that they have as much right to be here as we do. After all, they were here first. Humans are so different. We have money and expensive tools and we plan our work extensively before we start. Porcupines plan nothing and do everything with their teeth ... teeth that continue to grow if they don't grind them down.

The porcupine motto is pretty simple: if you want to stay alive, keep on chewing!

Bruce Day still owns "Heartwood"—his property near Markdale, Ontario—and spends as much time there as possible. He also enjoys hiking, canoeing and exploring the Bruce Peninsula and nearby Beaver Valley with friends and family.

One Little Ounce

Sometimes that's all you need.

By Barbara McAlear

Here's a little lesson proving once and for all that an ounce of prevention is definitely better than a pound of cure.

For many years our family owned a small cottage on an island located in Georgian Bay, Ontario, surrounded by beautiful white sand beaches and wonderfully clean water. Our neighbors, Frank and Diane, had a family of seven children and a shaggy mutt dog.

Island children, no matter whom they belonged to, were treated as extended family by most of the cottagers. We formed something of a loose-knit family: everybody was included in water-skiing events, corn roasts, card games, singing and dancing around bonfires in the sand, or playing silly word or number games while sitting around the campfire.

There was no television at the cottage, so adults and children learned to read and enjoy books. We happily learned about each other and watched our families grow up.

Because we were on an island, everybody had to pull together. If one cottager needed a plunger or a widget, they would inevitably find one at somebody else's cottage.

As it happened, Frank and my husband Al were sitting on Frank's deck one weekend chatting about his family's cranky septic system, which is a topic of long and thought-provoking conversation among cottagers everywhere. Due to the fact that Frank had such a large family, they had friends visiting nearly every weekend; as a result, his septic system was beginning to show a little wear and tear. My husband, being familiar with wells and water pumping systems, suggested that Frank should put a bit of yeast in the septic tank to activate it, which he assured Frank would get it going again.

Frank had never heard of such a thing, but readily agreed to give it a try. He and my husband took Frank's boat and sped off to the mainland village to pick up some yeast.

That evening, Frank waited until most of his family had gone to bed for the night before adding the yeast. Although my husband had suggested putting in only a few ounces, Frank figured that more was better, and therefore dropped in the entire package. He was going to make sure that he unplugged his septic system on the first attempt.

All was quiet and serene that next morning. At around ten o'clock, my husband and I decided to go for a walk along the beach. As usual, we met other cottagers on our walk and sat down in the sand to have a gossip, to watch the boats pass by, and possibly to cadge a cup of coffee while enjoying the beautiful sunny day.

It was at some point during this conversation that we heard an unusual rumbling sound building to our right. Everyone turned to see what was going on. Suddenly, from the point where Frank's cottage jutted slightly into the bay, we heard a massive explosion. The next thing we knew, a geyser had erupted from the back of his property, which began raining toilet paper and other "fragments" down over the roof of Frank's cottage and the nearby trees.

His septic tank was erupting!

At almost the exact same moment, every door in the cottage opened and began to spew out adults, children, and dogs, in various states of undress. All were craning their necks toward the sky to see what was going on. You might guess that some of the remarks coming from the cottage's inhabitants were unusually colorful.

Everyone else could hardly stand up, we were laughing so hard.

After the hubbub was over, Frank and family spent the rest of the day cleaning up the aftermath of his "pound of cure." But to this day, his family continues to suffer good-natured ribbing from their many island neighbors.

Barbara McAlear's family no longer owns the cottage on Christian Island, but they remember fondly the many family gatherings at their "home away from home." This is her second story for a Summit Studios anthology. She is also the author of "Blue Window Van," which appeared in Never Trust a Smiling Bear *(2010). Barb McAlear passed away in 2013.*

The Great Wall at Pelican Lake

And other ill-advised ideas.

By Ryan Clement

You've gotta love lakeshore property. You can always tell which lots in a new development are the lakeshore lots by the SOLD signs and high prices. In some parts of Canadian cottage country, lakeshore properties are such prized real estate that generations will spar over which branch of inheritors gets to come up on long weekends.

Our family was lucky enough to snag just such a parcel—a piece of waterfront paradise. Of course, my parents weren't exactly Fortune 500 people. Both were public school teachers who happened to have three things going for them. One, they didn't live in Southern Ontario. Two, they *did* live in Western Manitoba, a traditionally underpopulated part of Canada with affordable cottages (at least at the time). And three, my father was a bit of a handyman—or at least he considered himself to be one—who lived by the mantra, "If it ain't broke, fix it anyway." Thus, when my parents first came to inspect the lot during a January blizzard, they saw past the drifting snow, the leafless trees, and the frozen landscape to envision their future summer home perched on a ten-meter cliff overlooking the lake. What they didn't see was the unstable composition of the cliff itself and its unfortunate tendency toward erosion.

To be fair, my father did get certified as a journeyman carpenter. Eventually. But while he had aspired to be an engineer at first, he instead ended up as a building construction teacher at a local high school in Brandon. It was probably his desire to satiate lingering architectural urges, as well as to find a little getaway place not far from Brandon, that had brought my parents to the cliffside property down at Pelican Lake.

Once the property had been purchased, they decided to build their cabin out of the ruins of an old farmhouse that had once been used for storing grain—which explained our ongoing problems with inquisitive mice. The new cabin, with big windows and a screened-in porch, had a beautiful view of the lake. In true cottage fashion, my parents chose not to replace the paper-thin walls in the old bedrooms, probably so everybody could hear each other's snoring. The windows were angled perfectly so the light reflecting off the lake pierced your eyes each and every morning, and the floor sloped gently toward the bathroom so you could always find it in the middle of the night. They also built a loft, for no particular reason other than to have a perch where children could throw things at each other from above. It also provided a cramped but useful storage space, which was only accessible by a built-in ladder with rolling steps.

Our cottage wasn't as grand as some of the mansions that have sprung up around the lake in more recent years, but it's emblematic of our family—as clear as my dad's footprint, which is still visible on the ceiling because he happened to step on a piece of wood before putting it up. It wasn't easy to keep up, and often the property seemed like a continuous work in progress. Yet it was a place to try ideas that we dared not try at home. Some of them worked, some didn't. But all were worth a shot, even if a bad experience with a hummus toilet turned my parents off pita dip for life.

Neither side of the family was exactly new to the Pelican Lake area. My granddad, on my father's side, had actually come down to the lake as a summer camper in 1912, back when such traditions were just beginning. In those days, he got there by taking a train to Ninette; then he caught a ride on the seasonal paddlewheel ferry down to Y Point, where he and his cohorts promptly carved their names into the front of the general store. While I'm sure the storekeeper didn't appreciate the gesture, nothing was done to remove the vandalism. Almost a century later, the etching is still visible in the still-operating store, which gives you some idea of the lethargic pace of change around there.

My grandparents on my mother's side were among the first members of the Pelican Yacht Club, which was originally neither a club for pelicans nor a place that had any yachts. It was actually a dilapidated old one-room schoolhouse that had been moved to the outskirts of Ninette and populated by a group of nowhere-near-the-ocean nautical nuts whose philosophy was basically to throw a boat in the water and see what happens (a motto they still live by today). Homemade wooden sailboats called Fireballs—so named because of the speed at which they capsized—were all the rage back then. Everyone agreed that it was a fine way to spend a summer afternoon destroying your knees. We even have a few pictures of my grandparents in their old-style kapok lifejackets, which filled with water if punctured, meaning that at least your drowning would be quick.

Like Dad, my grandpa had also fancied himself a handyman—okay, he actually *was* an engineer—and in addition to building Fireballs and the occasional power plant, he also dabbled in totem poles. When my father first met his future in-laws, the two sides bonded over their mutually non-existent Haida heritage (I'm not sure either of them had even been to British Columbia) and carved an eight-meter wooden statue from a discarded telephone pole. It became a major landmark of nearby Curran Park, proudly declaring its cultural dubiousness for decades before deteriorating to the point that it threatened nearby children. Like most of the stuff we didn't know what do with, it ended up behind our Pelican Lake cabin, where the family tradition of crazy ideas best flourished.

Pelican Lake prides itself on being the largest navigable body of water in southwestern Manitoba, although that may or may not be true. My father, never a fan of the metric system, thought it was about a mile wide by thirteen miles long—approximately the shape of an elongated dog turd. In addition to various points that jut out into the water, there are only two real towns of note: Ninette and Pleasant Valley. Ninette is known for its gas stations, farming-based economy, vintage wild-west Main Street, and the remains of a picturesque turn-of-the century sanatorium that is rumored to be haunted. Pleasant Valley has a golf course. The entire lake is part of the Pembina River Valley system, so it's not so much a lake as one part of a narrow river that suddenly gets really wide. Despite being reasonably close to the small sandy desert of Spruce

Woods Provincial Park, Pelican is a lake of shale, shale, and more shale. Gray, crumbly cliffs tower on both sides—well, they tower compared to the surrounding Prairies—and are remnants of the great glacial river that once flowed to ancient Lake Agassiz.

At first glance, it's not the prettiest lake in the world. It doesn't have the boreal forest of Clear Lake up in Riding Mountain National Park, or the islands and sea-like expanse of Lake Winnipeg. Unlike the transparent tides of the aforementioned Clear Lake, or the burnt-brown tone of most lakes in the Whiteshell Shield country, Pelican Lake is a prairie lake. This means fertilizer runoff and other wholesome ingredients keep it pea-soup green for a good portion of the year. In addition to the toxic algae, however, one can find other flora and fauna here. In some places, deciduous trees line the shores and cliffs, providing channels between the farmland for wildlife to follow the river system. Porcupines, foxes, deer, cormorants, hawks, and even the occasional moose can be spotted. A flock of wild turkeys blocked our path to the boat launch just this spring, while last year I swear that I saw a wolverine.

While development has recently reached a pace approaching feverish—for this part of the country anyway—you can still find plenty of peace and quiet. Even on the busiest days of summer, the lake is large enough and long enough that you can usually find all the space you need, although you *can* expect the usual crew of pontoon boats, sailboats, and other craft drifting point-to-point in search of the next happy hour.

One has to be careful, though, as being sandwiched as it is between two parallel shale cliffs, the lake can become something of a wind tunnel. Storms can appear out of nowhere, and the long, dark stretches of thunderheads that we refer to as Witches' Noses send sailor and water skier alike bolting for shore. These weather systems crackle with electricity and have been known to spit out hailstones and even the odd tornado. Many a story has been told about naive visitors underestimating the ferocity of Prairie summer storms, only to be rescued by a watchful local with a smug, rain-soaked grin. To be fair, though, I know a couple of those same locals who've sunk their own fair share of boats all by themselves, which in a lake that gets no deeper than fifteen feet is actually something of an accomplishment.

While Mom and Dad certainly did—and still do—their share of cruising, most of my childhood memories of the lake involved moving boat hoists, building docks, patching leaks, and moving heavy cinder blocks to one place, only to realize after you'd done all the work that they had to be moved back to where you got them from.

But our biggest problem, by far, was the cliff our cabin was perched on. Every year we watched the cliffs erode further and further.

The problem was that the cliffs were pelted by storms all year long. Spring in particular sent sharp icebergs to gouge out holes at the base of our cliff. To make matters worse, there were often major changes in water levels from year to year. Some years, we'd have to install four or five lengths of dock just to get out into water deep enough to set up a hoist for our motorboat. Other years, we could basically launch from the base of our cabin's stairs. There are times when major changes would inexplicably happen overnight. It was not unusual to park a Sea-Doo on the beach for the evening, only to wake up the next morning to find it on dry land.

Eventually the problem got to the point where we had to do something about it. People were starting to talk about a cabin, described with many of the same features as our own, that looked like it might fall into the lake. While we didn't exactly stand at the bottom of the cliff trying to hold it back with our bare hands, some of our strategies proved equally as effective. Somebody suggested planting a grass lawn, but this just kept reminding us of how much turf we were losing. My mother tried planting trees and vines, hoping they would grow up and secure the cliff like the walls of an Ivy League school. But the local deer came by during the winter and ate them.

Next we tried fortifying the base during the off-season with our dock and boat hoist segments. Since our dock and homemade hoist system was an epic construction and deconstruction each spring and fall, pieces were constantly breaking off and likely someday to become fossilized at the base of the cliffs. Unfortunately, while our growing junk pile at the cliff's base did slow down some of the decay—and sometimes provided a home for wandering wildlife— it did not solve our problem. Not to mention that getting chased away by an angry muskrat whose home you've just "salvaged" doesn't make for the best start to a season.

Most infamously, my parents had the brilliant idea to "borrow" old fridges from the Ninette dump and use them to form a breakwater at the cliff bottom. While I pointed out that our neighbors might find the sudden appearance of a Stonehenge of refrigerators beside the public beach to be something of an eyesore, my mother assured me that they would paint the fridges to look like rocks. When I mentioned that rocks don't usually look like perfect rectangular cubes with built-in door handles, she told me to go to my room. They did actually manage to get one of the fridges down there, and it was a good four hours before the first environmental complaint came in. A grizzled resource officer with a gun on his hip ordered the fridge to be removed. Old fridges, you see, contain nasty chemicals like Freon, which aren't so great for the ecosystem. I suppose this is why old fridges are generally taken to proper waste disposal facilities and not used to prop up disintegrating cliff bottoms.

Of course, the biggest problem in our efforts to solve the cliff problem was the timing. We were only down at the cabin during the summer months, and there were only so many weekends in those. If the weather proved calm and sunny, it was great for water skiing and tubing, and the cliff had to take a number. If there was a little bit of wind, then there was no point in wasting a perfect sailing day. If it was cloudy and raining, then we'd drive to the nearby town of Killarney to patronize their discount stores and jump on the trampoline. That's not to say our working days weren't many: my parents always seemed to have a very long to-do list with projects in various states of completion.

We did eventually find a solution. It turns out that rocks—as opposed to fridges painted to look like rocks—actually serve as a pretty good buffer against the elements. Fighting our reluctance to adhere to straightforward solutions, we piled a series of rocks at the base of the cliff. They had the advantage of being ecologically friendly while at the same time not being edible or providing a good home for muskrats. And to our surprise, the barrier of rocks actually stopped the erosion!

The rocks are still there today. So are the cliff and the cabin that sits on top of it, where I am currently typing these words. We even have a nice earth-tone staircase now, which connects our cabin to the beach below, with guiding lights, handrails, and only the slightest bit of wobble. We've even unearthed the old totem poles, at the suggestion of our Sioux neighbors, who told us they should be placed at the entrance of our property in order to reflect traditional aboriginal customs. We decided this entrance was not our cabin's driveway, but rather the waterfront to greet incoming boats.

As tradition dictated, fishing the totem poles out, getting them down the hill, floating them over to the base of the cliff, and erecting them as a rain storm approached was just the kind of absurd summer ordeal that engenders our proud family tradition. It was a lot of work, it involved a lot of cursing, and no matter who counted "One... two... three!" no two people ever lifted at the same time. In the end, we got the poles in place.

As the rain clears, I spot neighbors aboard a pontoon boat floating down the lake, beckoning us to put down our fruitless labors for another day and join them for a happy hour that will last long into the evening. Summers are short in Manitoba and meant to be enjoyed. While it's true that work is an inevitable feature of owning any cottage, it is the time spent *not* working that brings families back year after year.

As his father would say, Ryan has been taking long walks off short piers at Pelican Lake since he was knee high to a clodhopper. His family has always been supportive of his writing, even if he occasionally "makes us look like screwballs." You can find Ryan's award-winning story "Hiking the Alps in Flip-flops" in the Summit Studios anthology Moose on the Loose *(2012). Or visit him online at* **www.clomy.ca***.*

Dandelions

Beauty is always in the eye of the beholder.

By George Brooks

Our grandson Julien and granddaughter Camrynne visit us often at our cottage home in northern Ontario. One year during the May long weekend, I was walking around the property with them, investigating what had changed since their last visit.

"Oh Papa!" cried Camrynne when we got close to the lake. "Look at all the beautiful yellow flowers!"

"Damn dandelions," I muttered.

"Damn dandelions, damn dandelions," mimicked seven-year-old Julien.

"Julien," I said. "I shouldn't have used that word. And neither should you."

"Damn dandelions," he said again, then looked up at me with an impish grin.

"Julien," I repeated sternly. "I'm giving you one warning." This was his parents' signal to him that misbehaving should stop.

Camrynne piped in again. "But Papa … they're so beautiful!"

I supposed they were to a five-year-old. She had no idea the hours I had spent pulling and digging out those offending weeds from the grass. The children let go of my hands and plunked themselves down on the ground, as only flexible children can.

"Papa, Papa ... sit down with the flowers," said Camrynne.

That was easy for her to say! The getting down part was not too bad; it was the getting up part that was difficult. Nevertheless, I managed to squat down and sit, accompanied by a fair amount of knee-joint cracking that brought a puzzled look to Julien's face.

Julien plucked one of the offending dandelions and I thought to myself: *Maybe I can trick them into picking them all.*

Camrynne picked another, a mature flower loaded with those pesky white wings that fly off with the wind to start more damn dandelions somewhere else on my property.

"Why are some of them white and some of them yellow?" asked Camrynne.

"Because they're old or dead," said Julien. "Like Papa."

I gave him a stern look, but not the "twice" warning. Camrynne was still looking at me with her bright eyes, waiting for an answer.

"Well, when the dandelions get old, the yellow blossoms turn into little white wings. At the end of each wing is a seed. The wind blows the seeds into the air and they float away. Eventually they land somewhere and start growing into a new dandelion."

"Is it like the birds and bees?" asked Julien. He had a silly grin on his face.

What has his mother been telling him? I thought to myself. *He's only seven!*

Camrynne looked puzzled. "What does Julien mean, the birds and bees?"

"Oh no, I'm not going there," I said, and started to feel a little hot under the collar.

"Birds and the bees, birds and the bees" chirped Julien.

"That's enough, Julien," I growled.

"Camrynne doesn't know about the birds and the bees," he continued.

"Julien, that's two warnings!"

We sat quietly for a few minutes. Camrynne plucked a white wing from the mature dandelion and studied it. "Is this the seed?" she asked, pointing to a dark spot at the end of the wing.

I gave Julien a nervous glance, but he seemed more interested in some dried leaves he had found on the ground. "Yes," I said. "That's the seed."

"Do all seeds grow into new dandelions?" she asked.

I pondered this for a while—as adults tend to do—instead of just giving a simple answer and saving myself a lot of grief. "I think most of them do," I answered cautiously.

"So some seeds die like Carli's puppies did?" she said. It was more of a statement than a question, so I let it just hang there.

"Are you going to die, Papa?" she asked. She looked at me with her big brown eyes, which were starting to fill with tears as if she already knew the answer. Julien stopped playing with the leaves and looked up at me apprehensively.

How do I get myself into these things? I thought.

I tried to sidestep the question. "Well, all things die eventually, but new life comes to replace whatever dies," I said. Both children gave me a quizzical look.

"What I mean to say is that when something dies it gives new life to something else. Like those dried leaves Julien has in his hand. They were green and alive once, hanging from a branch on that tree over there. They died and dropped to the ground. When one of those feathery dandelion seeds lands on them, the seed uses the leaves as food and grows to become a beautiful yellow dandelion." I almost choked on those last words. "So life starts over and over again. That's the beautiful thing about nature and life."

Julien and Camrynne stared at the leaves and then looked at the white-feathered dandelions in their hands. Camrynne gently blew on the mature dandelion and dozens of seeds floated away. "Have a good life," she whispered.

She said it so softly and sincerely that I had to say the same. "Have a good life."

At this poignant moment Nana called to us from the cottage porch. "I have some lemonade ready. Does anybody want some?" I raised my arm and gave a friendly wave.

The children jumped to their feet while I struggled to get to mine. I looked at the ground where I had been sitting. There was dog dirt from Carli. I looked at the back of my pants, which was now covered in it!

"Papa pooped his pants!" shouted Julien. "Papa pooped his pants!" Both children looked at me and laughed.

"Julien ... don't make it three!"

We started back toward the cottage. Partway up I stopped and looked back at the yellow blanket of dandelions. Something inside me must have changed, because they no longer looked like a blight to be torn from the ground and discarded. They looked beautiful.

I was just about to apologize to Julien for not seeing the humor in my plight when he looked up at me and solemnly said, "I'm sorry, Papa."

I gently squeezed his hand. How could I explain to him that I was the one who should be sorry? These intelligent and inquisitive children had reopened my mind to the beauty and wonder of nature. It was *me* who needed the count of three, not them!

They let go of my hands and ran toward the cottage. Before the screen door had swung open, I heard the children shouting, "Papa pooped his pants! Papa pooped his pants!"

George Brooks and his wife Susan love their cottage home near Magnetawan, Ontario, except for their battles with dandelions, mosquitoes, blackflies, and wild animal poop.

*Visit George's web page **www.tuskertheelephant.webs.com** to read some of his award-winning children's stories.*

Paddling as a Parental Tool

Or how to ruin your son's life for the rest of eternity.

By John Iannotti

Our family started paddling when my three kids were in their teens. One of our favorite family adventures was to paddle down Loyalsock Creek in our home state of Pennsylvania on weekends. We made it an annual family tradition, with picnics along the thirty-five kilometers of river that we usually covered. So when my oldest son Jeff and I needed to work out a conflict, it seemed appropriate that I use the paddling experience to build a bond between us.

A little background: Jeff was fourteen or fifteen at the time, and very conservative in his behavior. He was not a risk taker; in fact, he could easily be described as introverted. On the flip side, I am naturally gregarious and rarely see a risk not worth taking. We were at odds over discipline relating to some of his chores, but I don't remember exactly what the issue was. After all, he's now forty-two with three sons of his own, one of whom is very much like me.

We put in above Higgins Camp and floated down the river, arguing along the way about which parts of the creek to run. I wanted to hit all the big waves, while my son preferred to avoid them. Bonding was not going so well.

As we approached the swimming hole before a rapid called *Last Chance Saloon*, we faced a very big decision. To the right was my target: a narrow, fast-curving section of river with a large wave train beneath a rock wall. To the left was a very shallow section that rippled over small rocks for a bumpy but simple ride down.

Jeff tried desperately to paddle the front of our sixteen-foot Coleman canoe to the left, while I used rudder strokes to overpower him. There was no evidence of bonding at this time, and any witness would have seen an epic battle taking place.

As any canoeist would know, I easily won the battle for direction. But here's the thing: my son's strokes had left us broadside to the channel, and as we entered the Class III section I lost control of the canoe. We became airborne on the first of the sizeable waves, which quickly swamped the canoe and dumped us into the whitewater. We swallowed water as we rode the rapids down the remainder of the chute and into a swimming hole.

To our surprise there were a large number of teenagers frolicking in the swimming hole, including several classmates from Jeff's high school. We washed up on the shore across from them. My son had lost various items and had to dive for them in the swimming hole at the base of the rapids. Meanwhile, I bent over and began bailing out the water-filled boat.

When my son finally came back to the canoe, he looked very humiliated and very angry. He told me that we had to leave immediately. The teens across the river had stopped whatever they were doing and were now gathered together laughing and pointing at us; I guessed that their hysterical laughter was making him uncomfortable.

To prove my competency and regain some respect, I stood up in the back of the canoe as we paddled away. For some reason, the laughter increased. When I sat down and felt the very cold seat, I knew why. My bathing suit had torn open at the back and I had been mooning the crowd for several minutes while I was bailing out the boat. My standing in the canoe was an unexpected encore.

When I told Jeff, he gave me a look that turned from horror to extreme anger, then faded slowly to fear as he contemplated facing his classmates at school. He paddled harder than I thought was possible until we had rounded the bend and slipped out of sight of the applauding high school kids.

We rarely talk about that day without his face showing a range of emotions. I still enjoy telling the story, though.

John Iannotti is a retired engineer and manager who has been active in youth activities all his adult life. Having lost his father a month after birth he appreciated the importance of having a dad, so he got involved with Boy Scouts, Big Brothers and Big Sisters. He served in all capacities, but prefers the fieldwork, like camping in the jungles of Panama with his troops and paddling on the rivers of eastern Pennsylvania.

Newlyweds on the Trapline

Romance can be painfully elusive in the Alaskan wilderness.

By Michelle Bland-Bruce

Y ou have to hit the target dead on, or you're going to do it again. Do you understand?" That was my husband Ben, telling me in no uncertain terms that bear spray, jingle bells, and singing the Beach Boys wouldn't cut it out here. This was for real. This was Alaska. And Alaska has bears. Lots of bears. Today he was determined to teach me the finer points of handling a shotgun.

Ben crossed through the woods that circled our small canvas tent, which was hunkered between a stand of trees in the remote Alaskan wilderness. He took an old dog food bag, drew a large bullseye on it, and nailed it to a tree. As I backed up twenty-five meters and considered taking aim, he explained for the hundredth time that if a bear came into camp I needed to know how to use the shotgun. If a bear decided on visiting our camp for a free lunch, buckshot might be the only thing that would deter him.

I felt pretty sure I knew what I was doing. As a kid in 4-H, I had gone to the shooting range and shot at the clay pigeons. So what if I was twelve at the time? It was like riding a bike, right? I nuzzled the gun into my shoulder, looked down the barrel, took a deep breath, exhaled, and pulled the trigger.

BOOM!

The shotgun kicked like a horse and I winced. "Damn thing almost took my shoulder off," I whined.

"Shoot again," Ben hollered. "You didn't hit the middle. If that was a bear, you just pissed him off."

I hesitated. The shotgun's kick had hurt. Ben saw the look on my face and said, "A bear will hurt a hell of a lot more! Now, shoot again."

There was no way I was missing this time. I took aim, shot again, and hit the bullseye dead on.

"That's my girl! I knew you had it in you."

I smiled, proud of myself—and very grateful I didn't have to shoot again. My shoulder was still aching. Living on a remote Alaska trapline had its rewards, but it sure had its share of challenges, too. This was just one of the many new skills I had to learn to be prepared for daily living in the wilderness.

Ben and I were newlyweds, living one hundred and thirty kilometers from the nearest town. We'd moved to a remote trapline to mush dogs and live a simpler life. It was wonderful, but it was a huge change from the life I was used to. There was a time, just four years prior, when I had worked as a traveling college counselor for alma matter outside of St. Louis. I traveled the country staying in bed and breakfasts; my coffee came from the local Starbucks; and going out meant wearing heels and miniskirts. Now my coffee was percolated on a woodstove, and going out meant using the outhouse.

It was a change that I was ready for, and gladly accepted. I had always dreamed of living like my grandmother had lived—as a pioneer woman. Alaska was my opportunity to do just that!

Ben and I met in Bethel, Alaska, a small town eight hundred kilometers west of Anchorage. I was an elementary school teacher and Ben taught pre-school. We were surprised to have so much in common, and after just a few dates we had a pretty good idea that this was it! We shared a passion for living life, and craved change and adventure. Many of our first dates consisted of me following Ben on my snow machine as he mushed his dog team. We'd camp out for the night, and then mush back into town. After dating for a year, we got married in an outdoor ceremony, where I got to mush the dog team down the aisle.

Ben and I both dreamed of living remotely, so the trapline was a perfect fit; there would be no running water, no electricity, and no heated cabin. Instead, we settled in with our dog team, an eight man Arctic tent, and a large woodstove. The Alaskan wilderness was on our front stoop, with no interference. No cell phones, no television, no neighbors to make unexpected drop-ins, and no computers to distract us. For a couple of newlyweds, it was the perfect setup. Can you think of a more dramatic way to get to know your husband than by living in a day-to-day survival situation?

We spent our days caring for the dogs, trapping for our income, and hunting for our own food. We walked hand-in-hand down the frozen creek bed to look for fox tracks, spent afternoons panning for gold, snuggled into our sleeping bags when a blizzard set in, and hiked the nearby mountains looking for game.

Oh the days my husband was out trapping, I would see to the domestic duties around the camp: washing laundry, cooking meals, and so on. I enjoyed these activities, as they weren't mundane when done at camp; I saw it as a challenge. We had to haul water from the creek to drink, wash, and cook with. That, in and of itself, took a long time. Never mind that you had to heat it over the woodstove, adding an hour to an already lengthy process.

Doing laundry was the toughest, because you had to haul several pails of water for each wash. I began to get my arm strength up and could soon carry a forty-five-pound bucket of water the fifty meters back to our tent without having to stop for a break. Some might find this tedious, but the truth is, the day-to-day chores gave me a great sense of accomplishment because of the extra effort required to do them. At night my husband and I slept well, as we had spent our days outside and had worked hard.

All my friends joked before we left that I'd return the next summer pregnant, since we'd have nothing better to do on the trapline than fool around. Boy, were they wrong! I'll never forget my naivety about being a new wife. I figured we'd have plenty of time, too. But with no indoor plumbing it was tricky to bathe. Our official policy was to shower once a week, whether we needed it or not. And you can bet we did!

We were very lucky to have received a small portable shower as a wedding gift from some friends. Those friends certainly knew what a useful gift was. The shower had a tank that you placed on top of the woodstove and heated to the desired temperature. Then you used a pump to pressurize the tank, and finally used a small nozzle to spray yourself down while standing in a small basin next to the stove. You could muster about twenty seconds of water pressure before you had to pump again.

We bathed inside the tent because at minus-thirty degrees Celsius outside, the water would have frozen too quickly. (Not to mention the fact that it would have been a dreadful experience to be naked out there). It took at least two hours for the large tank of water to heat up to a warm thirty-five degrees. Plus, it required almost twelve liters of water to be hauled from the creek, which meant that bathing became an afternoon event.

My maid of honor had thrown me a very nice shower, where I had received several sexy nighties. One cold day while Ben was out running the dogs and checking traps, I decided it was time I pulled one of these nighties out of the bottom of the trunk to surprise him when he got home. I spent the afternoon hauling extra water so I could bathe, shave, and prepare for a special romantic night. I could hardly wait for him to pull up with the dogs. He would come home to find a hot, homemade meal on the table, the candles and lanterns lit, and his new wife wearing her finest lingerie.

This was what being newlyweds was all about! So what if it had been two months since we said our vows? We both knew that living on the trapline demanded some sacrifices, but tonight I'd make up for some of them.

When Ben pulled up with the dogs, I felt a sudden rush of excitement. Unfortunately, it was short-lived.

Ben hollered from outside for me to get my gear on—he needed my help. The tone of his voice indicated that I shouldn't dawdle, so I quickly threw on my long johns, fleece bibs, down coat, hat, gloves, boots and headlamp. I opened the door of the tent and saw my husband unleashing his sled bag. There was a dog nestled in it.

Without explanation, he asked me to put up the remaining dogs quickly, then to clear the tent table. We were going to have to perform some surgery.

As it turned out, two of the younger dogs had stumbled onto a porcupine and were absolutely covered in quills. We'd have to give them shots to numb them and then remove the quills before they lodged further under the skin.

By the end of the evening we had removed over ninety quills from the dogs, and they were both resting peacefully by the fire. It had taken us about five hours to remove them all, and we were exhausted. Dinner was cold, and I was ready for bed. I peeled off my long johns, took a look at myself in the lingerie, and sighed. Our romantic evening was never even mentioned; I didn't have the heart to tell Ben what I had planned. I would prepare it all again another time.

The next time came about two weeks later. Again I hauled extra water for a shower and shave, prepared a scrumptious dinner, lit some candles, and slipped into my special nightie. This time I felt sure we'd have the nice evening I'd planned.

Once again I felt a rush of excitement when Ben pulled up with the dogs. I peeked out of the tent, and Ben asked me to come and help put the dogs away. I wasn't worried, as he often asked for help. I dressed quickly and started for the door when I realized that Ben wasn't handling the dogs yet. He was still standing on the sled. Usually he had put two or three of them away by the time I got outside.

He had a large smile on his face and I was afraid my surprise was over. Yet his smile was mischievous. He was waiting for me to see something.

I took a closer look and realized that my husband's arm was covered in porcupine quills. We wasn't in too much pain, but it looked horrible! He'd shot a porcupine for dinner and had placed it on top of the sled bag. When he'd unexpectedly hit a tundra tussock, the sled tipped over, the porcupine fell off, and Ben had slid right into the damn thing.

Ben joked that it was the porcupine's last act of defiance. Little did he know that this porcupine was also keeping us from sharing a romantic night together. I spent the evening pulling over one hundred quills out of his arm.

Who would have thought porcupines could be such an effective form of birth control?

Michelle Bland-Bruce currently teaches ESL at the University of Kansas, where she enjoys sharing adventure stories with her wide-eyed students.

The Blob at Green Lake

All the neighbors were asking about it.

By Lisa Hatton

Our family owns a cabin in the Cariboo country of British Columbia. Located just east of 70 Mile House, it takes about five hours to get there from our home in Metro Vancouver. It's a lakefront property scattered with fir and pine trees, and when the weather cooperates it's an awesome place for having fun in the water. We used to have a floating dock that was rolled out into the lake and was used by swimmers, by sunbathers trying to tan, or for mooring the canoe or rowboat.

Back in the 1990s, my partner Bryon and I made many trips up to Green Lake. Since we both like to recycle as many things as possible, discarded items from home often found their way to our cabin. Couple this with having a combined four kids that ranged from their mid teens to their early twenties—all of whom appreciated new and unusual ways to have fun—and it provided the perfect incentive to create "The Blob."

Shortly after Bryon and I had set up house in 1994, friends who were downsizing gave us a king-size waterbed. We already had a king-size bed in our bedroom, so Bryon set up the waterbed in our spare room. Unfortunately, it filled the entire room, leaving no space for other furnishings. Shortly after the project was completed, my daughter Sarah asked if she could come to live with us instead of staying with her father. After we agreed, her next question was, "Can you get rid of the waterbed? There's no room for any of my stuff with that thing in there. I'll bring my own futon from dad's to sleep on."

So we drained the waterbed and Bryon salvaged all the wood from the frame for future use.

Two years later, as Bryon was cleaning out our garage, he ran across the empty waterbed. "Do you think they'll take the mattress envelope at the dump?" he asked.

"Why don't we take it up to the cabin?" I suggested. "We can fill it partway with water, the rest with air, and put it on the lake for the kids to jump on. You know, like on the video we watched from that summer camp." Bryon raised his eyebrows, but he agreed to keep it until our next trip to Green Lake.

On a Saturday morning in July, Bryon folded and stored the empty mattress in the back of his big F-250 pickup truck, along with a dirt bike, coolers, boxes of food, large plastic containers with clean sheets and towels, suitcases, and several red cans full of gasoline. All set for adventure, Bryon got behind the wheel with me beside him; Sarah and our two cats were relegated to the crowded rear bench seat. Bryon's two sons, James and Patrick, planned to drive up in another vehicle.

By midafternoon we had all managed the five-hour journey from Langley to Green Lake, and we were unpacked and ready to enjoy ourselves. After helping Bryon launch the dock, the boys took off on their dirt bikes. Sarah, now a languid seventeen-year-old, had slung a hammock and was catching some rays. I poured some iced tea and sat down on the porch swing so that I could look over the lake. Bryon was busy with his new project. He had set the pump up in the lake, attached a garden hose to it, and was now trying to fill The Blob with the required amount of water. The more water it ingested, the harder it was for him to hang on to it. So he attached some rope and tied it to a tree.

It was getting warm out, and by the time the boys returned from terrorizing some neighboring cattle, all three young people were ready to take a dip in the lake. After a beer or two and some reconfiguring of rope and dock, they decided it was time to try out this new adventure. Since there were no trees beside the lake with conveniently overhanging branches to swing from, the only solution was to run down the incline toward the lake and jump onto The Blob from the two-meter beach cliff.

Patrick went first. A short and slim sixteen-year-old, he hurtled down the incline with great speed before leaping into the air. He hit the mattress like a splattered bug on a windshield and, unable to hold on, he slid down into the water as The Blob shifted its considerable weight and flipped over on top of him. Undaunted, he tried several more times with the same result.

Eager to outperform his younger brother, twenty-two-year-old James volunteered next. James weighed in at two hundred pounds, so this was a big gamble on his part. He took a swig of beer, ran down the hill, and jumped off the edge. But instead of cushioning his fall like a pillow, The Blob acted like a trampoline and catapulted him far out into the lake.

He swam back to shore and wiped water from his dazed-looking eyes. "What happened?" he asked.

"You must have hit it at the wrong angle," said Bryon. "Try again. I'll hold it for you so that it doesn't move."

After James had ricocheted into the lake several more times, Bryon rethought his original design. "I think it has too much water in it. I'll let some out. Maybe we should pump some air into it instead."

Unfortunately, with that much water inside the mattress, there was no way to siphon it out while it bobbed in the lake. The only solution was to drag The Blob up onto the beach, high enough so that gravity would allow us to drain some of the water. Fortified by beer, Bryon and the boys labored industriously to move the water-laden mattress up the incline. It was hard work.

It was close to suppertime by the time they finished their task. Clouds had darkened the sky and nobody wanted to swim anymore, so we all went into the cabin. After eating, we could hear the wind lashing the treetops; coming back from the outhouse, Bryon confirmed that it was also raining. With a fire in the stove we were mostly content to stay indoors and play cards and board games. Except for Bryon, that is. He disappeared without telling anybody where he was going.

I thought he had gone to chop firewood. His boys thought he was visiting a neighbor. By ten o'clock I was ready for bed and starting to worry about him, so we phoned the neighbor's cabin. They hadn't seen him. Armed with flashlights, the boys checked outside our cabin and came back to tell me that both the rowboat and The Blob were missing. The Blob had been tied to the tree and the rowboat had been tied to our dock. It was impossible to see anything out on the lake in the dark, or to hear anything with the wind gusting and the waves breaking so loudly.

"Don't worry," said Patrick. "He can swim." He and James laughed nervously.

An hour later we heard footsteps on the deck. Bryon burst inside a few moments later, soaking wet and shivering.

"You'll never guess what happened!" he said. "That stupid mattress came loose and started drifting down the lake in the wind. I couldn't just let it go. So I got in the rowboat and went after it. When I caught up to it, I tied it to the boat and started rowing back. Do you have any idea how hard I had to row against the wind, pulling that damned thing back up the lake? It must weigh a ton!"

"Why didn't you just let it go?" I asked, more concerned about losing my honey than losing The Blob.

"What? After you made me bring it all the way up here? No way! I'd have had to row twice as far in the morning to go looking for it. And besides, we have to try it out with less water in it." He smiled sheepishly as he popped the top off a beer.

The next day Bryon couldn't persuade anyone to jump onto The Blob. But word must have circulated, because vacationers from up and down the lake came by in canoes and motorboats and Sea-Doos to ask about it.

By the afternoon, Sarah had found a new use for it. She took a book and sprawled on top of The Blob in a skimpy bikini, sunbathing and waving at any young males who were passing by. It was undoubtedly the largest air mattress on the lake that year, and it was the first and last time The Blob made an appearance at Green Lake.

In the 1980s, Lisa Hatton wrote a newspaper column for the Aldergrove Star about life in the community. She also enjoys writing poetry and short stories. Two of her eBooks—Love Found *and* Fire—*have been published on Kobo Books. She has taken many funny and eventful trips with her husband and family to their cabin at Green Lake. In addition to the story included here, she has written countless others that she hopes to one day publish in a collection titled* Honey Signed The Waiver. *Learn more about Lisa at* **www.ramsheadwriters.ca**.

The Outhouse

It wasn't the farewell they'd been hoping for.

By Erin Ruddy

When you grow up with a cottage—a place where you spend summers frolicking in the jungle gyms of nature—it becomes a part of you. It morphs into a sanctuary where every tree has a memory and every rock a special story to tell.

Like so many cottages back then, ours was rustic and filled with eclectic 1970s furnishings. It sat at the bottom of a long, disheveled driveway in Ontario's Haliburton region, overlooking a lovely bay on Little Kennisis Lake. There were no modern amenities at our cottage and the mosquitoes were downright nasty. But despite those inconveniences, it was a summer utopia—a place where a kid could run barefoot and free. We chased frogs, picked wild berries, fished with homemade rods, and roasted marshmallows under the black, starry night sky, which in those days did not have to compete with the glow from cell phones. It was a place where snapping turtles skulked and occasionally sunned themselves on semi-submerged logs.

Our cottage had been a labor of love, built by my grandfather in 1972. Poppa had maintained it with attention and care until the upkeep had become too much for his aged hands. With so many cousins, aunts, and uncles in the mix, you'd have thought somebody could have taken over the chores, or we could have split them in an equitable manner. But we couldn't. And so we decided to sell the cottage, the place we treasured more than any other place on earth. It was a sad, sad day for all of us.

For purposes of closure, each family was given the chance to visit our cottage one last time before the new owners took possession. My gang consisted of my mother Lynda, brother Joel, nephew Josh, me, my husband Brad, and our six-month-old baby boy, Nathan. Our final visit turned out to be a beautiful weekend replete with fall splendor, which we spent exploring down memory lane and reminiscing over the many incredible summers past. Oh, the adventures we'd had!

By noon on Sunday the party was over. It was back to reality as everyone gloomily headed off for home. I was the last to leave with my mother and baby. Ours were the final eyes to scan the property, to batten down the hatches, and to wipe away all traces of our family's unforgettable thirty-year history. It was the heartrending end to a memorable chapter in our lives. But it was time to say goodbye.

As we were about to leave, my mother said, "I have to use the outhouse one last time. Then we'll be on our way."

Moments later I heard a terrible shriek like none I've ever heard before. In a flurry, my mother burst out the rickety green door, looking paler than a ghost. Had a mouse climbed up the hole and bit her on the backside?

No, it was actually worse than that. She had dropped her keys down the outhouse hole—the car keys and key to the cottage included.

"What are we going to do?" she shrieked.

The situation did seem grim. We were three and a half hours from home, with no cell phone reception and no way to get inside the cottage. Not to mention that the autumn sun was waning quickly.

I glanced over at Nathan, who was sound asleep in his car seat and blissfully unaware of our predicament. Then my gaze turned back to my mother, who looked possessed and desperate, her eyes darting madly from tree limb to tree limb.

"I'll have to dig them out," she finally said. "Maybe I can fashion some sort of hook out of twigs or something…"

As she scurried off into the woods, I decided to check the cottage for open windows; I knew full well that all of them were securely locked, because I had done it myself. Then I heard something—a loud disturbance coming from the cottage next door. I walked through the trees to see what was going on and found a group of men—they must have been renters, because I didn't recognize them—who were laughing and carrying on as they cooked dinner over an open flame.

I felt a surge of hope. These men would surely know what to do! They were fishermen after all, and fishermen always come equipped with tools and ideas.

It only took me a few seconds to realize they were drunk.

"Good day!" one of them shouted gleefully as I approached. Then the expression on his face changed. "You don't look so happy."

"No," I said. "I'm afraid I have a problem."

After I explained what had happened, the men stared blankly at me for several long seconds, their jaws hanging open in disbelief.

Finally the burliest fellow, who seemed to be the ringleader of the group, said, "Sounds to me like you're up shit's creek without a key!" This was followed by an explosion of hoots and laughter.

"I have a *baby*," I said firmly. I knew it wasn't their fault we were in this predicament, but I think I might have glared at them.

That got their attention. An infant was involved, which meant this was serious business.

"Well, we'd better get over there and have a look," the burly man said. He got up from his chair, and so did his three friends, who followed him through the trees armed with tackle boxes and fishing rods. When they reached the outhouse they found my poor mother standing inside, with a stick lowered into the pit.

"Excuse us, ma'am," said the burly fellow. He gently pushed her aside. To our amazement the four inebriated men squeezed into the tiny cubicle and got down to business, trying to devise a mechanism that would pluck our keys from the pit.

"What size hook you got?"

"Nope, mine's better."

"Whatta load of crap!"

"Who's got a flashlight? I can't see nothing in here."

I would like to say that these men were the Dream Team of outhouse key snatchers, but that would be an exaggeration. But they were helping us, and for that we were grateful. Given that the keys weren't even visible, I gathered that the plan was to somehow sink a large hook down into the pit, swish it around and hope for a snag.

We tried to be patient as they fished and rooted for the keys, but they never did make contact with the coveted item. The problem with fishing for keys, of course, is that no bait—no matter how shiny or flashy the lure—will encourage a bite.

After many long minutes the team leader looked defeated. He swiped the surface of his glasses with the cuff of his dirty sleeve.

"How heavy was that clump of keys?" he asked.

"There were maybe eight or ten keys on the ring," my mother said.

"Good Lord. We're gonna need some heavier jigs."

"Or a coat hanger," my mother suggested.

It was as though a collective light went on.

"That's a great idea. It's sturdy and we can unravel it for extra reach."

"I'll go fetch one," said one of the men.

"Grab a fresh round of brewskies while you're at it," chortled the drunkest of the bunch. One of the men staggered off into the trees and returned several minutes later with the requested items.

As I eyed the coat hanger I couldn't help but wonder about their plan. "How are you going to lower it in there?" I asked. But the big guy had already taken charge of the situation. His shirtsleeves were already rolled up and his head was bent in concentration. It looked like he was preparing to dig into the raw sewage with his bare arm.

I couldn't stand it any longer.

"Stop!" I said. "Please, stop." He looked at me over the rims of his glasses, which were fogged over with steam.

"You don't want me to get the keys out?"

"Yes," I said. "But there has to be another way."

Suddenly, my mother came barreling down the driveway

with her cell phone waving in the air. "I got him! I got him!" she shouted. "He's coming!" She explained how she had climbed atop a boulder and managed to get just enough cell reception to call her husband. He was now making the long drive north with the spare key.

Then the funniest thing happened. The men who had been helping us—despite the fact that they were now free to go—seemed disappointed. It was like they were hardwired to reel in any fish, and we had just deprived them of landing their most challenging catch yet. So, with splattered faces and reeking with the unmistakable odor of *Nuit du Outhouse*, they shuffled back to camp and went straight for the beer cooler.

"Thank you!" we called after them as they disappeared into the darkness. "Thanks so much for trying!"

It was pitch black by the time my stepfather David arrived. Exhausted and drained of all nostalgia for our cottage, we climbed into the warm car and headed home.

We laugh about the incident now: the crazy debacle that overshadowed our big, teary farewell. But we've learned a few things from this and other incidents. We've come to realize that laughter is the best medicine, the cure-all for everything. We still miss our cottage, but we've also learned that in the end it's not our possessions that matter most. It's the people in our lives and the experiences we share with them.

Oh yeah, and we've learned to never take our keys into the outhouse.

Erin Ruddy is a professional writer, editor and weekend warrior who divides her time between the urban jungle of downtown Toronto and the calm glory of Northern Ontario. When she is not at work pounding out business articles, she can be found sneaking off into dark, quiet corners to try and wrap up her first novel, a work of fiction that will take readers on a thrilling odyssey into the wilds of Northern Manitoba.

The Pig Roast

*Never provoke redneck who holds carving knife
in hand.*

By Barbara McAlear

Every year in September we receive an invitation from our
friend Bill to attend a pig roast at his home marina in Port
Perry, Ontario. About fifty or sixty friends and family members—
many of them with boats—congregate at this annual barbecue. For
that reason, everybody is expected to bring a potluck dinner dish
to share, plus plenty of liquid libations to keep the party going.
Our family usually brings several dozen husks of corn, and then a
bunch of us gather round and tell stories while shucking the corn
and stuffing the leaves into big green garbage bags. My husband Al
and I also rent a propane corn cooker as part of our contribution to
the event.

Chef Bill is a dyed-in-the-wool redneck, though I've always
thought of him as a shy extrovert. He loves his family fiercely, but
has nevertheless created nicknames for them: his loving and tolerant
wife Kay is "Bertha," his charming son Kevin is "Peckerhead,"
and his kind and gentle daughter Lisa, who inherited her father's
infectious smile, is known as "Fred."

Bill was once a lanky six-foot-two, but has grown a beer belly
over the years, which is framed by his red suspenders. He loves his

houseboat to distraction and cares for anything old and precious. For breakfast, he often eats a chocolate delight called a Joe Louis and takes a generous shot of booze in his coffee, which fuels him through the day until cocktail hour.

One memorable year, the weather was holding onto the remains of a hurricane that had not quite finished drenching everything in sight. The men had set up a tent-like tarpaulin and were trying in vain to keep everybody dry. But for hardy mariners, who are used to being wet, that is not a big problem; a few sailors' rums and we had all joined together to scoff at Mother Nature's best efforts to put a damper on our day. Young people and elders alike were huddling and cuddling, trying to keep warm and dry under the leaking roof.

I must tell you a little of the marina's layout, so it will be easier to understand how the following incident came about. A creaky wooden boardwalk about five feet wide runs along the water's edge beside the covered boat slips. This boardwalk forms a V shape along the triangle of land, which allows boats to dock on both sides of the land jut. In the center area there is gravel and some scruffy tufts of grass, and on top of that sits a picnic area and playground where children can run wild and free.

Our group had assembled the pig barbecue and corn cooker in the middle of this area, about twenty feet back from the point of the V. When we arrived, the barbecue was already huffing and chuffing away for all to watch, smell, and drool over. The pig was progressing nicely, dripping fat into the fire and causing a melee of crackles. The aroma was intoxicating.

The meal began coming together quickly. As we cooked the corn, the rest of the food was stacked up on trestle tables, covered with plastic sheets weighted down at the corners with washed rocks the children had collected off the beach. Chef Bill was flamboyantly sharpening his knives, waving them in the air while at the same time keeping a judicious eye on the roasting pig. He was waiting for the perfect moment to take it off the spit and transfer it onto the carving table for dissection. For this purpose, our chef and his handy helper had propped a picnic table covered with a foil wrapper onto the edge of the boardwalk, while the other end rested on the ground. This tilt of about eight to ten inches was evidently to make carving the pig as convenient as possible.

It was finally time to take the pig off the barbecue. Bill and his helpers lugged the hundred pounds of succulent meat over to the picnic table and cautiously drew out the spit. Our chef had a smile on his face and was swaggering about despite the fact that his eyeglasses were fogged up and his sopping hair was plastered to his forehead. He was waving his machete-sized knife around like a swashbuckling Musketeer.

Bill inspected the pig carefully to confirm that it was as perfect as he had been proclaiming. By this time almost everybody was huddled under the makeshift canopy, eagerly awaiting the feast. I was hovering to the left of the picnic table, watching the spectacle as the chef approached the pig with his knife. He severed the trussing wires, then retreated back slightly to admire his sizzling, bronzed offering. Judging by the glow on his face, one would have thought he had killed the pig with his bare hands.

As Bill paused to prepare for the butchering, a husky young man who was new to the scene came trundling up the boardwalk. He walked up to the rear of the picnic table, lifted a leg and nonchalantly dropped his foot onto the seat at the far end. His considerable weight caused the table to pitch violently, which catapulted the pig into the air. We watched with horror as the pig flew across the boardwalk and splashed into the murky water between two boats.

"Stunned" is such an inadequate word to describe the look on our chef's face. His eyes grew large and his head canted forward with shoulders raised as the pig's trajectory replayed in his mind's eye. He was ominously quiet.

The newcomer took one look at Bill—with his machete carving knife clutched in one hand—paused for the briefest of seconds, and then turned and plunged into the water fully clothed. A few moments later he surfaced with the hundred-pound pig in his arms and awkwardly deposited it onto the boardwalk.

Time was suspended. Nobody dared exhale as we waited for Bill's response.

The chef walked calmly over to the still-steaming pig, studied it, and grabbed a hose that was coiled on the nearby walkway. He gently washed it off, lifted it onto the table, and went on to carve it as though nothing out of the ordinary had happened.

The funniest part: Most of the guests, too caught up with their own laughter and conversation, hadn't even noticed what had happened. Kudos went around to Bill for his culinary genius.

A boat owner came over later and mentioned that his boat seemed to have a ring around it from some sort of oil spill. There were a couple of knowing winks exchanged between the helpers, but nary a word of explanation was offered.

Chef Bill has since made the trip up to the big restaurant in the sky, which was far too soon for those of us who knew and loved him. We all miss him very much.

Barb McAlear's family owned a cottage on Georgian Bay's Christian Island for many years. She is the author of "Blue Window Van," a short story that appeared in the Summit Studios anthology Never Trust a Smiling Bear *(2010). She also wrote "One Little Ounce," which appeared in* Moose on the Loose *(2012) before being reprinted in this collection of stories. Barb McAlear passed away in the spring of 2013.*

The Joy of Fishing

Everybody should experience such bliss.

By Frank Brummet

The sun was just cresting the treetops when I reached the lake. A faint breeze was rippling the water, just enough to break the perfect glassy surface. Small fish were jumping near the shore and further out I could see a few big ones rising. It was a perfect day: one of those days that fishermen dream about.

Although it was mid-June, the early morning air was cool and I was glad to be wearing my heavy jacket. By the time I had rigged up my rod and was ready to begin casting, the sun had reached the lake and rainbow trout were rising and feeding everywhere. I would catch my limit in a few hours; I was certain of it.

My first cast was a good one. The hook, worm, and float went out and out and farther out still. It might have been the longest cast I had ever made! The rest of my line, however, had only traveled about three feet. I realized that I had forgotten to flip over the bail on the reel, so out there in the middle of the lake was my best float—now irretrievable—along with a prized worm hanging from it. It would be a free lunch for the first fish to spot it. Of course, that fish would no doubt be a monster.

I kept my eye on the float while I was rigging up again and, sure enough, about two minutes later it dipped beneath the water.

I watched the float bobbing and jerking as it slowly moved toward the far side of the lake. Damn! It was frustrating to lose my best float. No matter; I had three spares and I reminded myself that it was still an almost-perfect day.

In the trees behind me several squirrels were chattering, scolding me for invading their territory. A short distance down the shoreline a group of whisky jacks were watching me, telling each other that I would probably eat my lunch soon. They would then close in on me, begging for any scraps that I might throw their way. These birds can be very bold when they know food is present, and will noisily and persistently shame you into sharing with them. I ignored them and returned to the business at hand.

On my fifth cast, the float had hardly settled when it suddenly disappeared and my rod tip snapped down. It was a big one! I set the hook and proceeded to play the fish. The surface of the water exploded as the rainbow jumped three feet into the air. He looked like a two-pounder, for sure. I played him patiently, letting him run with my line several times, all the while slowly coaxing him toward the shore.

Five minutes later he was within reach of the net. As I bent over to pick it up, my plastic cigarette case fell out of my top jacket pocket, landed on a rock, and popped open. Cigarettes scattered all over the water and mud. But there was no time to worry about that; landing the fish was more important!

Carefully, I steered the fish toward my net and scooped it under him. He gave one last desperate twist and the hook whipped out of his mouth. The end of my rod snapped up, which caused one of the hook's barbs to connect with the end of my thumb.

"Aaaaarrgghh!" I shouted. I dropped the net and my rod. I stood there in shock as the fish flopped out of the net and into the mud, then bounced into the shallow water before flashing away into the depths of the lake.

For several minutes I cursed the fish and his entire family, with special emphasis on the questionable virtues of his mother.

When I ran out of breath, I suddenly remembered my dropped cigarettes. Looking down, I saw that I had stepped on most of them, grinding them into the mud. The ones I hadn't managed to step on were slowly sinking under the water, completely saturated. Perhaps this was the day I would quit smoking.

I must have been shouting rather loudly, for when I chanced to look around I noticed that the whisky jacks had retreated a considerable distance along the shore and were silently huddled together on a huge boulder, casting nervous glances in my direction. The squirrels had ceased chattering and scolding me; indeed, I was sure I detected a faint whimpering from the topmost branches of a nearby tree. One small branch was trembling. Across the bay a loon was cruising in circles, slowly shaking his head.

After a few minutes my heart had ceased pounding and my hands were almost steady. Only my throbbing thumb reminded me that I had a surgery to perform. The barb of the hook had penetrated the skin and was completely hidden from sight. I knew that gentle pulling and wiggling would never remove it.

There was only one thing to do.

I always carry a small set of needle-nose pliers to remove hooks that are deeply embedded in a fish. It had never occurred to me that someday I might have to use those pliers on myself. As I gripped the hook with the pliers I closed my eyes, took a deep breath, and yanked up as hard as I could. The resulting shock of pain was indescribable. It felt as though I had pulled off my entire thumb! Nevertheless, since the throbbing had increased tenfold, and since it came from the vicinity of my thumb's tip, it was safe to assume that my thumb was still attached to my hand.

I slowly opened my eyes. As I did so, I could see a trail of blood running down my thumb toward my wrist. The hook had torn out a large chunk of flesh.

I stooped down and swished my thumb back and forth in the lake. The icy water felt like a hundred stabbing needles. Then, in an attempt to stop the bleeding, I stuck my thumb in my mouth and repeatedly spit out the blood.

I remember thinking: *Is this how vampires get started?*

After about ten minutes of sucking and spitting, cursing and mumbling (yes, the cursing had started again) the blood flow had finally slowed to a trickle. I dug into my tackle box, found a dusty, crumpled bandage, and wrapped it around the ugly wound. Thank goodness there were no other fishermen on the lake. They would surely have been shocked and sadistically amused to witness a semi-senior citizen cursing and mumbling, shaking his fist at the lake and sucking his thumb between utterances.

Then—ignoring the dark premonition of more disaster to come—I stubbornly decided to continue fishing. After all, what more could go wrong?

The following hour was spent casting and retrieving without a single strike. I couldn't believe it. Surely there must be *one* hungry fish out there.

Although it was only ten a.m., I decided to eat my lunch. I needed a cup of coffee. I searched the shoreline, found the dry forked stick I had used on previous occasions, and stuck it upright in the mud. Then I made a long cast, laid the rod in the stick's fork and sat down to eat. If a fish chanced to strike as I was eating, I would only be a couple of meters from the rod and could reach it in an instant.

After one bite of my sandwich the action started. The float went under and the rod bent almost double. The dry stick apparently couldn't take the strain of such a hard strike because it splintered in two, and my rod fell into the mud.

Unfortunately that wasn't the end of it. The line had somehow managed to loop itself over the handle of the reel so that instead of the tension pulling line off the reel (as normally would happen), the fishing rod and its assembly were pulled toward the lake.

Dropping my sandwich, I jumped up and lunged after it. I stumbled into the water up to my knees and just managed to grasp the last few inches of the rod handle before it disappeared. I raised the rod and leaned back to take up the slack in the line. Big mistake: my boots slipped on the algae-covered rocks. Before I could say "whippersnapper," I was sitting waist-deep in the icy water. The fish had snapped the leader, of course, and the line hung slack from the rod's tip.

I should mention that I am usually a reasonably well-coordinated person. However, the fishing gods obviously had other ideas for me on this particular day, as my "perfect day" had become a nightmarish series of muddlesome mishaps.

With this thought in mind, I crawled out of the water and stood up to ascertain what further havoc had been wreaked. The sandwich I had dropped was now a mud sponge. The remainder of my lunch was a flat, disgusting mixture of crumbled cookies, squished cheese, mushed meat and mangled bread—victims of my size thirteen boots. To complete the disaster, I had managed to kick over my open thermos bottle, and my precious hot coffee was by then a slowly sinking puddle in the grass.

It was time to take honest stock of my situation: I was soaked from the waist down, my boots were full of water, and my thumb was throbbing like a jungle drum. I was hungry, cold, craving a cigarette, and had not yet landed a single fish. Furthermore, I was shaking violently, partly from the cold but mostly from anger and frustration. The sensible thing to do would be to go home quickly, immediately, before I caused *serious* harm to myself.

I threw my unused worms (a lot of them) out into the lake—hoping as I did that any opportunistic fish would choke on them and die a slow and painful death. I left my mangled lunch for the whisky jacks, assuming they could stomach it. Shaking and shivering uncontrollably, I broke my two-piece rod into three pieces, stuffed them into the rod case and jammed the reel into my tackle box. As I was about to leave, I spotted my backpack leaning against a bush; I had almost left without it. Then, without a backward glance, I squished and sloshed along the trail with my boots still full of water.

On the way out I met another fisherman who was just coming in to the lake.

"Hi there!" he said with a friendly smile. "Any luck?"

I cannot recall exactly what happened next. But when the wall of red had cleared from my eyes, I saw that he was sprawled on the ground, glaring up at me and holding the left side of his face. The contents of my tackle box was strewn in the dirt beside him. I can only guess that I had thrown a punch at him with my right fist; his misfortune was that my tackle box was in my right hand at the time.

Rather than burden you with more unpleasant details, suffice it to say that I have been ordered to appear in court next month to answer for assault charges. Last week I sold my boat. My rods and tackle I gave to my sons. I believe that they, too, should have the opportunity to experience the joy of fishing.

Frank Brummet has been writing stories and poems for more than twenty-five years, and has had several poems published by the Poetry Institute of Canada. He is still hoping for a humorous encounter with BC's legendary Ogopogo.

Kojo's Island

He looked like a laughing Buddha.

By Chris Czajkowski

To understand Jun's story, you have to know something about me, and you have to know something about wwoofing. Wwoof: no, it has nothing to do with dogs, or stereo speakers. And wwoofers are not (it is to be hoped) "people who throw up in the floatplane," as the owner of Tweedsmuir Air at Nimpo Lake calls them.

This reference to floatplanes is significant because that's how most people get to my place. The only other way is to hike for anywhere between fourteen hours and three days, a lot of it over unmarked virgin forest, swamp, and tundra.

Twenty years ago I made my first trip out here, on foot and alone, with the idea of building a cabin. The British Columbia government has laws against people simply heading into the boondocks and squatting, so I had to have a commercial reason. Ecotourism was to be my savior: that was the only thing suited to the high, harsh climate of the region I had chosen. The water was frozen for half the year, and the winds that barreled down the lake from the 12,000-foot spine of the nearby Coast Range were often so severe that all exposed trees leaned sideways. This was a small thing I had neglected to notice when swept up by the magnificent views, wine-sharp air, and glorious solitude of my first August visit.

Two years and two months later, a day after I had finished screwing down the metal on the roof of my first cabin, the worst recorded windstorm in living memory passed over northern British Columbia. With fear and trembling I huddled in my sleeping bag beneath the thrumming metal (my tent was long gone), terrified that my roof would go and along with it all my dreams. I knew that whatever I planned to do there, if I survived at all, would be forever dictated by that invisible, fickle, and implacable aeolian battering ram. Which is why I called my new home Nuk Tessli; it means West Wind in the Carrier language, and is a reminder of who is boss.

For the first decade I operated alone. It took me three summers to build the first two cabins. The ground was too uneven and rocky for a wheelbarrow, let alone horses (if there had been any closer than 40 kilometers away), and the only machine I had was a chainsaw. I hauled the logs with a come-along and a peavey, and raised them with a block and tackle. The building "leftovers" were used as firewood. My carpentry was crude—my furniture-making father would have turned in his grave—but the buildings were warm and dry inside and stood up to the storms.

After the building waste was consumed in the stoves, I had to find other firewood. I felled dead trees with the chainsaw, bucked them up, rolled the stove-lengths to the waterfront, and split them into manageable sizes. Then I loaded them into my canoe, paddled them home, unloaded, and hauled them up to the woodshed. I used firewood for both cooking and heating, but rarely used more than three cords in a year—the equivalent of about six full-sized pickup truck loads. Still, collecting and preparing it was a monstrously slow job that took weeks.

I also began to brush out a few trails for easier access to the alpine regions, in anticipation of the tourists I hoped would start beating a path to my door. After all, it was only a twenty-minute floatplane ride from Nimpo.

The wilderness surrounding my home evoked superlatives. The cabins stood at 5,000 feet, and sprawling wildflower meadows were only 1,000 feet higher. Nearby mountains peaked at 8,500 feet. A slow trickle of tourists did come, and I guided and cooked where necessary. But with the buildings complete, I had lots of time to explore. Many of my ramblings were in the high country—on foot in the summer and with snowshoes in the winter. Once every four to six weeks I would make the trek to the nearest post office at Nimpo Lake, a journey that might take a day in summer if I was lucky, and usually took three in winter.

I was not at Nuk Tessli all the time. I needed to earn money, so I planted trees in the spring and presented slide shows in the fall to promote both my ecotourism business and the books I had written by then.

By the time I was fifty, I figured the business warranted another cabin. But I no longer had the energy of a decade before. As luck would have it, three young Germans—friends of friends—wanted some wilderness experience. They were tremendous workers; one was skilled as a builder and could already use a chainsaw. Having so much help with that building was a very different experience than my solitary struggles with the first two. So when one of the young Germans said casually one day, "This would make a great wwoofing place," and suggested I apply to be a host, I embraced the idea with open arms. It was a decision that has significantly changed my life.

W.W.O.O.F. is an acronym for Willing Workers On Organic Farms. It's a worldwide operation that connects small-scale farmers with travelers. Opportunities range from harvesting organic rice in Japan to growing kiwi fruit in New Zealand or digging carrots in Lillooet, BC. Not that I have an organic farm. I am lucky if I can grow a crop of radishes at my altitude. But the organizer of WWOOF Canada told me it didn't matter.

And so into my life came a steady stream of usually young (but not always) people of both sexes from Germany, Switzerland, England, Belgium, Canada, Australia, New Zealand, Korea, and Japan. I warn prospective wwoofers that the work is physically hard—a few of the early ones found it more than they bargained for—because life at Nuk Tessli is not exactly like tending a small vegetable plot. Luckily, the majority have flung themselves into the heavy physical labor with great enthusiasm.

Junsuke Ishizu had spent three months in Calgary learning English before he came to me, but Nuk Tessli was his first ever wwoofing experience. He had come well stocked for a month's stay: in the guest cabin to which I had assigned him, and to which I went after the day's tourists had left, were strewn a multitude of clothes and possessions. There was a small, tinny radio with CD player, a dozen throwaway cameras, a tottering pile of Japanese cigarette cartons, and a large bottle of vodka. Alcohol was a big part of his life; he later showed me pictures of his friends, always at parties and always absolutely plastered. Indeed, I found out later that a serious hangover had almost caused him to miss the tourist plane to Nuk Tessli. During his sojourn with me, however, I never once saw him overindulge in alcohol, nor complain about the lack of it.

Clothes-wise he was not so well prepared. His Nikes were not rugged enough for the rocky terrain and swamps he would be expected to work in; his pants were too new; and his crocheted hemp hat was of very loose construction, each hole a perfect conduit for the mosquitoes to reach his freshly shaven head. So I let him rummage in the spare clothes box and he found a complete outfit down to a pair of gargantuan boots that he was forced to stuff with extra socks. The pants he favored were castoffs of mine, relegated to the box after I had put on too much weight. They were so baggy on him that they barely clung to his hips, but he thought they were *really* cool.

Jun's English was not too bad. He spoke rapidly and with confidence, if not with a great deal of precision. Overall, he communicated well. The day he arrived was pristine: a deep blue sky reflected in the lake and soaring snowy mountains rising high to the west. Jun stared at this scene, enraptured.

"Can I swim?" he asked.

"Of course," I replied. "But it's cold."

"Can I ... Can I ... naked?"

"No problem," said I.

Gleefully, he thrust a disposable camera into my hands, flung off his clothes, and waded into the lake. "Take picture for my Mom," he said.

Jun was as green as they come as far as "practical" work went. Most Asian visitors to my wilderness seem to be this way. They live deep within large cities, without the remotest connection to anything natural. Apparently, Jun lived in a suburb with a garden and a dog, but he never helped with the gardening. His mother worked in a bank.

Jun had absolutely no idea of the relationship between his food and the environment. He did not know, for instance, that birds ate berries. He had never canoed. One day I brought along my fishing rod and caught a fish, and when I showed him how to gut and clean it, a caviar of insects spilled out of the stomach cavity. "Fish eat flies?" he squeaked with such alarm that I doubted he would ever eat fish again. (Actually, he said "fries." Like most Asians, he had difficulty with the *l* and *r* sounds.)

Needless to say, his experience with any kind of tool before he came to Nuk Tessli was zero. He clutched his first axe with both hands as if it might fly out of his grip, lifted it a few centimeters, then brought it down with a gentle tap onto a firewood round. He looked quite startled when it bounced up with barely a mark. I gave him a few pointers and left him to it. He struggled for an hour or so, then stuck his head into my cabin. "Enough?" he asked hopefully. But his small bundle of sticks was barely enough to cook a single meal, so back to the woodshed he had to go.

For all of Jun's slim build, he could, like most wwoofers, pack away large quantities of food. When he first arrived I also had to give him a couple of lectures about waste. Nuk Tessli is far from stores; I must shop for the whole summer in May, and if we run out of an item, it's usually difficult to replace. My first complaint, for instance, was the large puddle of maple syrup he left swimming on his plate. I did not mind how much he ate; but waste, I told him firmly, was not to be tolerated.

He learned, of course, just as I learned from him. After he had been with me for a couple of weeks, we were visited by an American who had a summer cabin at Nimpo, and who occasionally dropped by Nuk Tessli in his own plane. He left us with a large melon—an unprecedented treat—so we both hacked off generous slices and tucked in. But Jun left a good inch of flesh on his rind. At once I reminded him of my "no waste" policy.

"Excuse me," he said, "but in my country we have a lot of melons and it is not polite to eat right to the skin. If I did that, they would call me a yucky boy. Is very bad manners."

I apologized, of course, whereupon Jun eyed the half-eaten melon slice and said, "But I am in Canada now." With that, he picked it up and cleaned it off.

Jun's main job at Nuk Tessli was brushing out trails. I wanted to extend the existing trail that ran along the north shore of my lake past the portage, running it along the next lake that was just upstream. For the more distant areas, we worked together. Jun was a novice canoeist who could not swim, so although he learned everything quickly and listened carefully to what I said, I did not want him venturing too far on his own. Once he understood what was expected, he could paddle up the lake to the nearer section, take lunch and cigarettes, and stay there for the rest of the day. It was probably more solitude than he'd ever had in his life, so it can't have been easy for him. But he never complained. Not even on the day he saw the bear.

I have two dogs, both SPCA specials, and both (by coincidence) Rottweiler-colored. Bucky, in particular, has quite a lot of ginger on his legs and head. When Jun came home that night, he said he had heard an animal creeping through the thick brush, apparently trying to sneak around him. By bending down, he had glimpsed the animal's feet. "They were not thin and pointed, like deer," he said. "They were thick with long hair and flat feet. Same color as Bucky's feet. I think it was a bear."

I laughed and told him it most certainly was a bear. "What did you do?" I asked.

"I went back to the canoe. I stayed long enough to smoke two cigarettes. Then I went back to work. But I was frightened. I was singing."

I thought this was both very brave and very sensible of him.

"What language did you sing in?" I asked.

"Japanese" he replied, surprised at my question.

"That's no good," I told him. "It's a *Canadian* bear. It can only understand English."

Canoeing activities in particular are always dictated by *Nuk Tessli*, the West Wind. One morning a gale was blowing. Jun was not naturally an early riser, and considering it was too windy for him to canoe up the lake, I walked over to his cabin to tell him he could stay longer in bed. That was when I discovered something—sleep was not the reason he came late to breakfast. He was meditating. He and his family belonged to a Buddhist sect and every morning, and sometimes in the evening, he spent an hour chanting a mantra. In front of him, on the table, was a little pouch attached to a leather thong. He had been wearing it like a necklace when he arrived.

Jun spoke often of his mother and he was obviously very fond of her. Now he told me of his father, who had died very suddenly just before Jun had come to Canada. It was obvious that Jun was still having a hard time coming to terms with this. He showed me a picture of a chubby man with a large grin, who looked like a laughing Buddha.

"He was a very popular man," said Jun. "Very well respected. One thousand people came to the funeral."

Jun had decided to cancel his Canadian travel plans, but his mother insisted he continue. She had visited him in Calgary, bringing him his stock of strong Japanese cigarettes; he had begged her for them, saying Canadian cigarettes were too weak). She had also brought with her some of her husband's ashes. Jun had deposited little bits in places that he had enjoyed in Canada, and the remainder now lay in the little pouch on the table. He asked me if he could leave them at Nuk Tessli.

"Of course," I said.

His first choice for a site was one of the many peaks that surrounded my lake, but it was already the end of September and the weather was not going to let us get far above the treeline. So he chose one of the islands that form a loose ring about my cabins.

From it he could see the peaks he had scrambled up earlier that summer, the area where he had been working, the cabins, and the permanent snows that cover the 12,000-foot giants beyond the head of the lake. It was already windy as he launched the canoe, paddling jerkily across the water. He pulled the canoe on shore and I could hear the waves slapping and bumping it erratically against the stones. The sun was behind him and Jun's slim figure was silhouetted against the sky as he built a small cairn. He then made his farewells, the ragged strains of his chant scattered by the wind.

Jun flew to Nimpo a couple of days later. He hugged me on the wharf, and there were tears in his eyes when he said, "My father's name is Kojo. Speak to him sometimes, will you? Otherwise he will be lonely."

And speak to him I do. Kojo's Island is in front of the lowest point in the horizon as seen from my home, which happens to be the place where the sun rises on the shortest day. As the long, purple shadows of the island's wind-bent trees fan out toward me, I know that the darkest days of winter have passed and spring is on its way. It is an important day for me, for I am very much a creature of the light. And in that small way, Kojo's shrine remains a symbol of hope.

Many wwoofers have come and gone from Nuk Tessli, and all have left their imprint in different ways. But only Jun has left me the spirit of a man who looked like a laughing Buddha, and the memory of the son who mourned him.

Chris Czajkowski is an artist and author of several bestselling books, including Cabin at Singing River *(Camden House, 1991), the story of building her first log cabin 43 kilometers from the nearest road. This story was adapted from her book* Wildfire in the Wilderness *(Harbour Publishing, 2006). Chris sold Nuk Tessli to Doron Erel and Sela Bocovetsky in 2012, who still run wilderness expeditions from the location. To learn more about the Nuk Tessli alpine experience, visit **www.nuktessli.ca**.*

Deserting the Nest

Going to the cottage alone was all part of his master plan.

By Greg Simison

My son and daughter had devised a plan to go out to our cabin this weekend and rough it for a few days. As usual, at the last moment something else came up for my daughter and she opted to go camping elsewhere with some friends. I suspect the "something else" had to do with a good-looking guy who was joining the group for the weekend. As it's been since our distant relatives crawled out of the primordial ooze—in my family's case only a few generations ago—the opportunity to spend time with a potential mate overcame any sense of guilt about standing up a sibling.

Much to my surprise, instead of ranting, raving, and threatening to commit sistercide, my son just shrugged and said, "No problem. I'll go out there alone for three or four days."

I suddenly found myself staring at a sixteen-year-old kid who was exhibiting an amazing degree of maturity. But I didn't let that get the better of me. Teenagers are capable of acting like responsible adults one moment, only to drop down on the floor while howling and kicking their feet in a perfect imitation of themselves in mid-tantrum at three or four years old. And I'm an expert on that subject—a middle-aged man who does a great job of throwing tantrums when anyone says "no" to me.

Now it was decision time. Would I let my son go alone and prove that he's a responsible person? Or would I tell him I didn't think he was old enough to be out there by himself? Of course, I knew perfectly well that if I tried to stop him it would result in him moping around the house for the next three or four days, picking his teeth with his switchblade, and in general making my life miserable. It was an easy choice. I let him go. Sure, call me irresponsible. But you can't call me stupid.

My own parents encouraged me to get out into the world at an early age. They didn't believe in keeping me tied to their apron strings—well, just my wrists, and that was to stop me from flailing around too much as I was shoved into the trunk of the car. To this day I have dark memories of them tossing me at the side of some deserted logging road and urging me to be a man and find my own way home. "It's character building," they shouted as they roared off in a cloud of dust. To this day I can hear the echoes of their hysterical laughter and those joyful whoops bouncing off the steep mountainsides. However, their elation was always replaced by a deep depression when, weeks later, I inevitably staggered through the front door.

The truth is, I don't worry much about the ability of my kids to take care of themselves. I've always encouraged them to leap from the nest and try out their wings at every opportunity—except where their flight paths collide with mine. Both of them are street smart. The problem is, in the case of this trip to the cabin, the boy would be heading into a somewhat street-less environment.

Although he spent most of his first eight years living out in the boonies with me, when you live away from that lifestyle for a few years you tend to forget the skills you once possessed. For instance, would he remember not to soak the kindling in gasoline before placing it in the woodstove? Would he recall, as a five-year-old, watching me run screaming from the cabin toward the lake with the gasoline can still grasped in my hand, the top half of my body aflame like the Olympic torch?

Would he remember the lessons I taught him about the wildlife? "And that's why, Alex, you should never try to pick up a rattlesnake. Now, see if you can pry those fangs out of daddy's hand, will you?"

Is the lesson he learned about the questionable wisdom of feeding bears reinforced whenever he looks at my left sleeve pinned at the elbow?

Would he remember the safety tips he learned while watching his father during his younger years—such as how to safely use an axe and five-pound maul? Or would he only remember the aftermath? "Hey dad, I found another one of your toes on the other side of the woodpile. And look here, the rest of them are still inside what's left of your bedroom slipper."

Would he remember the rules of water safety? Can he still dredge up the memory of that red canoe disappearing beneath the waves while his dad muttered, "I guess you can't attach a large outboard motor to these things." Did he take the time to read the safe-boating pamphlet the search and rescue technician handed him as his partner performed mouth-to-mouth resuscitation on his blue-faced father?

I suppose it's too late to worry about such things now. At the time of this writing he's been out there for three days, and the police have yet to arrive at my door to ask if I'm the idiot who sent his slow-witted son out into the wilderness alone.

As for my daughter, she managed to make it home in one piece from her camping trip, moaning about bug bites, the "stupid scenery," and complaining about the poor quality of today's camping gear. "That stuff I borrowed from you was useless. You should take it back to the store for a refund. As soon as we lit our fire it melted right through the floor of the tent. And that double sleeping bag? It's far too small for two people." I didn't ask for additional details on the latter complaint.

You know, the more I think about it the less I worry about the boy. We haven't heard of him meeting with disaster yet, and perhaps he displays a lot more wisdom and maturity than I give him credit for. After all, in the end he somehow managed to get his trip in without the company of either his sister or his father.

It's almost as if he had planned it that way.

Greg Simison lives in Moose Jaw, Saskatchewan. His fifth book, Miscellaneous Wreckage, *was released by Thistledown Press in the fall of 2014. Since writing Deserting the Nest, both of his children have done just that. Greg still spends much of his time at lakeside cabins, with the local coroner's van perpetually on standby.*

Revenge of the Golf Bag

Somewhere in the Muskokas, somebody is losing their mind.

By James Osborne

Alex was an avid golfer who loved the course near his Muskoka cottage. One day he organized a game for himself and three of his neighbors.

Right from the first tee, it was obvious that one of the players was in trouble. Dick was second to tee off and he fanned on his first swing. He took a mulligan on his second. Four-letter words were already flying.

By the fifth tee-box, another member of the foursome, Jack, began to wonder about his cart mate. The other two golfers, Alex and Rob, were keeping as much distance from Dick as possible. They were feeling sorry for Jack, having to sit alongside Dick and endure his endless stream of profanity.

Dick's play continued to deteriorate hole after hole. The worse he played, the more agitated he became—it was a vicious circle. Early into the back nine, Dick began borrowing golf balls from Jack to replace those he'd driven into water hazards or far into the rough.

It just wasn't Dick's day.

Miraculously, the foursome managed to make it to the tee-box on the fifteenth hole. It was a long par four with a gentle dogleg around a large pond to the right. Alex was still leading the group with the lowest score, so he was first to tee off. Jack went second, Rob third, and Dick last.

By now, Dick was in a decidedly foul mood. His extreme agitation made it difficult for him to set his tee straight enough in the ground to keep the ball from rolling off. Finally he managed to do it. He took three practice swings. Then he stepped up to the ball and swung. The club head barely grazed the ball, causing it to dribble six feet from the tee box. Another string of profanity burst from Dick's lips. He took another mulligan and set the ball back on the tee. On the second swing, his driver connected solidly with the ball. It sailed out forty yards before slicing sharply to the right. The group watched with dismay as the ball dropped swiftly and splashed into the pond.

The men weren't surprised that yet another spate of profanity erupted from their angry colleague's mouth. But they weren't prepared for what happened next.

To the dismay of his golf mates, Dick threw his driver into the bushes beside the tee box. Then he jumped into the golf cart and sped off, leaving his bewildered cart partner Jack without his golf clubs. Jack exchanged glances with Alex and Rob. Without a word, they headed down the fairway to where their balls had come to rest. Jack was on foot, carrying his driver, which was the only club he had.

They fully expected Dick to drop another ball by the water hazard and take his shot—as the rules allowed—and then come over to pick up Jack. That wasn't to be.

"Uh-oh!" Jack said, drawing the attention of the other two men. "This isn't good." They looked across the fairway. Dick was unbuckling his golf clubs from the cart.

The three could hardly believe their eyes when Dick lifted his golf bag high over his head and threw it as far as he could into the pond, clubs and all. Then he jumped into the golf cart and sped off toward the clubhouse. Jack stared in disbelief as he watched his golf bag and clubs, on the back of the golf cart that he and Dick had been using, disappear down the fairway and over a hill.

"Go ahead and use mine," Alex said, offering Jack the use of his almost new graphite clubs.

The three had just finished their second shots when they saw Dick and the golf cart coming back in their direction. Jack's clubs were still on board. The three decided to be gracious and welcome Dick back to finish the game.

But instead of heading their way, Dick drove the cart to the edge of the pond and stopped.

The next thing they knew, Dick was removing his shoes and socks. Then he jumped into the pond and waded out to where his golf clubs had landed. They watched him as he thrust his arms deep into the water and swung them back and forth in searching motions. Finally he stopped and pulled his golf clubs above the surface. He began digging through the pockets of his golf bag.

He had obviously found something. The other men watched as Dick put it in his pocket and waded back to shore. Water dripped from his soaked pants as he picked up his shoes and socks, jumped into the golf cart, and drove back toward the clubhouse.

Alex, Jack, and Rob looked at each other, shrugged, and continued with their third shots.

They learned later that a furious Dick had arrived at the clubhouse, stormed out to his car, and only then realized that he'd left his car keys in the golf bag.

James Osborne is the author of two novels and more than seventy short stories, many of them set in cottage country. His award-winning stories have been published in regional, national, and international anthologies. While he's lived in cities out of necessity for most of his career, Osborne's heart remains in the country. Read more of Osborne's stories at **www.jamesosbornenovels.com**.

Siren Eyes

When traveling with your husband greatly lowers your life expectancy.

By Leslie Bamford

The wind howled. The sailboat bucked and wallowed. As I clung to a rail in the sailboat's cockpit, the wind whipping hair into my eyes, I looked up at my husband Bob. His face was set in a grimace, his hands tightly gripping the wheel. The ice-cold water sprayed over us and the sailboat was heeled so far over that I thought it was going to turn belly-up.

We were on vacation and I was about to die. Again.

"You have to experience sailing in the North Channel," Bob had said when we woke up that morning in our quaint Gore Bay motel. "Seeing the North Channel by boat is an absolute must if you want the real Manitoulin Island experience."

Needless to say, the trip was Bob's idea. He had started wearing me down in the winter while the snow was still covering the ground at home.

"Let's get back to nature," he had said. "What could be better for a summer holiday?"

His first choice was Manitoulin Island, land of Gitchi Manitou, the Great Spirit. Set between Lake Huron, Georgian Bay, and the North Channel, Manitoulin (as Bob reminded me) is the largest freshwater island in the world.

"You'll love it," he said. "There's fabulous scenery, and we can visit before the bugs come out." He waved a pamphlet for the Chi-Cheemaun ferry in my direction, his blue eyes flashing with excitement.

I should have known those blue eyes were luring me, like Sirens, to my demise. Bob's enthusiasm for trying new things always seems to involve me and a life-threatening activity. But I never see it coming. So from the safety of our living room that January, I ignored the sinking feeling in the pit of my stomach and agreed to go.

*   *   *

After a week on the island, Bob's promise of beautiful scenery was still in question. Mind you, it was hard to see *anything* through the constant sleet and snow. But he was right about the bugs: there were none to be found on Manitoulin Island that June. It was too bloody cold. Mount Pinatubo in the Philippines had recently erupted, which unbeknownst to us had spread a haze of sulfuric acid into the earth's atmosphere, blocking the sun and lowering temperatures worldwide. We packed bathing suits and sunscreen, but spent the first week of our vacation wearing parkas and mitts to stay warm in the near-freezing weather. When it wasn't raining, it was snowing.

Lesson learned: never travel with a Siren-eyed man if a volcano has recently erupted.

The morning we went sailing, the sun had come out for the first time in a week. Throwing off our parkas and mitts, we donned shorts and T-shirts and went outside. It was still cool, but the June sun had warmth in it, and we eagerly walked around Gore Bay Harbor looking for an appropriate place to buy some breakfast.

"Let's charter a sailboat today," Bob said. "They sail right from here."

Before I could think of a suitable reply, Bob whisked me into the office of North Channel Charters. Sounds official enough, I thought—no doubt a professional organization that's out of our price range, and unlikely to charter a boat to the likes of us anyway.

The office was actually a shamble of boat parts, papers, charts, and ashtrays full of cigarette butts. Behind the counter, a pudgy man in denim overalls was talking on the phone. He waved to us and went on talking. After ten minutes he hung up and asked how he could help us.

"We want to charter one of your sailboats today," said Bob.

The man and Bob discussed boats and prices while I tried to find something in the office to feign interest in, without any luck.

"Will you be our captain?" I heard Bob asking the man.

"Sure will," he replied. "And you'll love the boat. She's a thirty-four-foot Catalina. Perfect for a sail in the channel. Come back at ten. We'll be out for about three hours, round trip."

Before I could object, the captain swiped Bob's Visa card and we were back outside in the sun. Bob was smiling from ear to ear.

"Let's go back to the lodge and put on our bathing suits," he said.

"Are we going swimming off the boat?"

"Hell, no! The water is barely above freezing—you'd probably die of hypothermia if you went swimming for even ten minutes. We'll sunbathe. On the boat."

The words "barely above freezing" and "die of hypothermia" stood out in my mind—the water sounded like a death trap waiting for its next victim. But I tried to focus on the boat. I like boats, at least conceptually. Not that I'd ever been on a large sailboat. Or any sailboat, for that matter. Just a Hobie Cat (a small two-hulled boat, or catamaran), on another vacation when Bob had tried to kill me.

"What should we take?" I asked. "Food? Jackets?"

"We'll only be gone for three hours and we just ate, so I don't think we'll need any food. I'm sure they'll supply snacks, anyway. And look at the weather. It's beautiful! Who needs a coat? Sunscreen is more appropriate. And maybe some sweatpants and a sweatshirt to put on over our bathing suits if it cools off later."

Lesson learned: never listen to a man with Siren eyes when there is sulfuric acid in the atmosphere.

Just before ten, we walked over to the office of North Channel Charters, which is when things took a turn for the worse.

"I won't be your skipper today after all," said the man in the overalls. "Something came up. My son is going to take you instead." He waved his hand toward a scruffy kid sitting at the end of the counter smoking a cigarette. The kid looked about twelve.

"Oh that's fine," said Bob, holding out his hand to the boy. "My name's Bob Bamford and this is my wife Leslie. And you are?"

"Mors."

"Pardon?"

"Mors."

When the man in overalls saw Bob's raised eyebrows at the boy's incomprehensible grunt, he intervened. "That's my son Maurice," he said. "Named him after Rocket Richard. Man, could that guy skate. Maurice got the name but not the speed. Likes to sit around way too much."

He looked at his son, then back at Bob. "Teenagers ... what are you going to do?"

He turned to Maurice, who was still sitting on the stool. "Time to go, son, while the weather holds. Chop, chop. And remember to be back in three hours."

We followed Mors as he shuffled in his flip-flops along the dock toward a large white boat. He wore creased beige shorts and a white T-shirt with stains on the front. A pack of cigarettes bulged out of one back pocket.

Once we were on board, Mors started the engine and instructed Bob on how to assist with the mooring lines so we could cast off. Soon we were motoring out of the harbour. The water was calm and the wind was light. I slathered myself with sunscreen and settled back on the cockpit cushions to soak up some much-anticipated rays. In the background I could hear Bob making conversation with Mors about raising the sails; each question of Bob's was inevitably followed by a two- or three-word answer from Mors.

Soon Mors turned off the motor and raised the sails. We were sailing.

Mors put the winch handles in their holders, then gathered up the excess lines and tossed them down the companionway in a heap.

Bob turned to me. "Not ship-shape, throwing the lines below like that," he whispered. "Be careful you don't trip on them."

"Why don't you just tell him?" I whispered back.

"He's the skipper," replied Bob. "He's in charge. Sailing etiquette, you know."

I didn't know, and I didn't particularly care. I was just happy that it was warm and peaceful. Water lapped against the boat. Finally I could relax.

Mors steered while Bob and I lay in the cockpit. After an hour I sat up and looked around. We were sailing in the middle of a large body of water, with land on both sides. I peered into the distance to see what kind of cottages people had around here. I didn't see any; both shorelines were undeveloped. There were no cottages, no docks, no other boats, no people. Not even a bear fishing off a rock. We were alone in the middle of nowhere.

"We're going to a place I've always wanted to see," Bob said, leaning toward me in the cockpit. "The Benjamin Islands. They're made of pink granite. Mors says we'll love them."

I found it hard to imagine Mors saying anything of the kind, but who was I to spoil the look of bliss on the face of a Siren?

"Are we there yet?" I asked, noting that we were just about halfway through our allotted time.

"Almost," said Mors.

At the end of our second hour we were still not there. But the sun was still shining and my Scottish nature enjoyed the fact that we were going to get more than our money's worth out of this charter.

The wind began to pick up just as some islands came into sight about half an hour later.

"The Benjamins!" Bob exclaimed. He was beaming. "See how narrow the channels are between them? We're going to sail right through those channels."

He waved a chart at me. "These islands are called Sow and Pigs and The Boar. Isn't that cute?"

Adorable, I thought as I smiled back at him.

"If you haven't run aground, then you haven't been to the Benjamins," offered Mors, a cigarette hanging out of his mouth.

"What?" I asked.

"It's an old saying in these parts. Don't worry, it's fine. I know how to navigate. There's a dangerous section coming up."

Bob and Mors took down the sails, and then Mors began to turn the wheel—first clockwise, then counterclockwise—as we motored between the rocks. Suddenly his expression darkened and he tossed his cigarette overboard.

"I'm not sure ..." he muttered.

Bob looked at the chart, looked at Mors, then looked at the chart again. "I think we should be further to starboard," Bob said.

"I don't know," said Mors again.

"Haven't you done this before?" Bob asked. His face was serious now.

"Never. I just turned eighteen. This is the first time my father sent me out on a charter."

I looked at Bob. He looked at me, then back to the chart. "Over to starboard, Mors. NOW!"

The boy turned the wheel. Rocks were visible just below the surface of the water. I held my breath as we maneuvered between huge granite shelves in the narrow channel.

"We made it," said Mors, who looked visibly shaken. He brought the boat around a couple of islands, then back out into open water through a wider channel. He and Bob raised the sails again.

"I'm going below now. You can sail the boat, Mister."

"Can you get us a snack from down there?" I asked.

"No food on board, ma'am."

"Oh, well, a cold drink then."

"No drinks, either."

Mors went below. We'd been out for four hours now. The sun had faded behind a bank of clouds and the wind was steadily picking up.

Within minutes, the sky was dark and the temperature had plummeted. The wind began to howl and the boat heeled over at a dangerous angle. I scrambled for our sweatshirts and sweatpants while Bob steered. Mors remained below, sitting at the table and smoking cigarettes. The wind off the frigid water blew right through our clothes and soon I was shivering from both fear and the cold. We were in a dangerous environment with a novice who had never been out by himself, and we had no idea what we were doing.

The boat heeled over further as large waves began to rock the craft.

"The boat's falling over," I said to Bob as I hung onto the cockpit railing. "Make it stop."

"It's not falling over, it's heeling over," Bob said from his position at the wheel. "It won't tip. It's designed to do this. If you want to get back to Gore Bay today, we have to sail like this. I can't make it stop without sailing in the wrong direction."

"I'm scared," I said. I could feel panic rising in my stomach. "We're sinking, I know we are. We're going to fall out and drown. Or freeze to death in that water."

At that moment, several loud bangs echoed from below deck. Terrified, I looked down the companionway, expecting to see a hole in the bottom of the boat. Instead, I saw pots and pans skittering across the floor. Doors to various compartments were opening and closing. Mors sat at the table, smoking furiously, staring into the void.

Gingerly, with my head down to avoid flying objects, I went below and collected the pans, stowing them inside cupboards and making sure the latches were properly shut on all the doors. Mors wouldn't even look at me. The boat rocked and bucked, making it difficult to stand up. The lines Mors had thrown below earlier snaked around the floor, grabbing at my ankles, tripping me several times.

I was just getting the hang of avoiding the lines when my body was tossed from one side of the boat to the other and slammed hard against the bulkhead. As I attempted to reorient myself, I felt a sharp pain in my shoulder. My head could understand what had happened, but my stomach could not. Bile rose in my throat.

"I'm going to be sick!" I moaned.

Mors emitted a huge puff of smoke.

"SICK!" I yelled.

Mors pointed to a doorway. I opened it. A peculiar-looking contraption stared back at me, something that resembled a toilet, but different. I hesitated as I tried to imagine how it worked. Then I heard Bob calling, "Come back up. You'll get sick down there."

I looked at Mors again. He was chain-smoking, lighting a new cigarette from the old one. Apparently he had been blessed with a cast-iron gut, but few other redeeming qualities.

I climbed back up into the cockpit, stumbling as my feet got caught in the lines again. The air hit me like a blast from the Arctic and I began to shiver again.

"Good work down there, stowing those pots," said Bob.

"Go to hell," I said.

"We'll be okay. I can do this."

"Have you ever sailed a boat like this?"

"Well no, but …"

"Maybe I should just jump off and get it over with."

"Take the wheel."

"No bloody way."

Just then, a gust of wind came out of the sky like a giant hand, grabbing the Catalina and pushing her down. I saw the water coming up at us, saw the sail falling. I waited for the smash of the mast against the water. At the last second, the boat popped up like a cork, righting itself.

"What the hell was that?" I gasped.

"The wind almost knocked us down. But did you see what happened? It didn't." Bob gripped the wheel more tightly and focused. But I couldn't hear him. Or *wouldn't* hear him. Fear of death had intervened. I sat shivering, waiting for the next blow-down. The one that would be our last.

My thoughts raced. Who would have guessed I would meet my maker on the North Channel, land of Gitche Manitou? Me, a big-city girl who never intended to have anything to do with nature. I was more of a five-star-resort-and-swimming-pool kind of gal.

I shivered, waited. Then I felt a presence, something beyond the sky, waiting along with me. Waiting for me? I knew that the only way to get to that presence was to die. And I knew I didn't want to die. Not today. Not ever, really.

"Take the wheel," Bob said. "It's the only way to stop being afraid."

I looked at Bob, hating him, hating boats, and hating wind and sails, and boys who smoked, and God. Especially God. For making us die to find Him.

"Please," said Bob. "I'll hold it with you. Just try it for a minute."

I forced myself to stand up and squeeze behind the wheel. I put my hands on the icy chrome and held on. Bob held it too. I felt something. A tension. A connection of some kind.

"I feel something," I said. "What is it?"

"It's the sail, the keel, and the angle of the wind," said Bob. "Now turn the wheel to port a little bit." I turned to the right. "No, port is left," said Bob, guiding my hands. "Feel that?" I turned to the left and felt the tension on the sail lessen. "Now keep it like that for a few minutes, but then you'll have to turn to starboard again to stay on course. The boat will heel over more. Try it."

I turned the wheel to the right and the tension came back. The boat leaned again, but this time I could feel the keel keeping her from tipping over. I could feel it through the wheel, through my hands, through my body. I could feel the safety of the boat's design, doing exactly what she was made to do.

I looked at Bob. He was sitting in the cockpit. I was sailing the boat.

After a while I stopped gripping the wheel like I was strangling it. I stopped shivering. I stopped hating Bob, hating boats, and hating God. I even stopped hating Mors.

I stayed at the helm for two hours until Gore Bay Harbor came back into view. Then Bob took over. Mors emerged from his sweat lodge below deck to help me take the sails down and direct Bob to the North Channel Charters dock.

Bob brought the Catalina into her slip like a pro, leaving Mors gaping in admiration, his tobacco-stained mouth open.

"I think Mors was terrified out there," Bob said under his breath as we tidied up the lines.

"His father should never have sent him out with so little experience," I said. "He could have run the boat aground."

"But he knew when to listen and he did what I said. Best of all, he let us sail the boat!"

"Spoken like a true Siren," I said.

"Huh?"

"Never mind."

"We ought to thank him," said Bob. "He needs to hear something positive before his father tears a strip off him for being gone seven hours instead of three."

"Just don't breathe in when you get close—he's probably still exhaling."

Before we clambered off the boat, Bob approached Mors and said, "Good job out there, buddy." He patted Mors on the shoulder and shook his hand.

"Bye, Mors," I said. "Thanks for everything." I offered my hand and held my breath. His grip was damp and limp, but he smiled at me for a second before turning and plodding toward the office and whatever retribution awaited him. I found myself hoping his father would go easy on him.

Bob turned to me. "Let's go, honey. I'm buying you a gigantic martini. To celebrate."

"To celebrate what? Another near-death experience?"

"All you needed was two minutes at the wheel and you were hooked on sailing. I saw your face. Come on, admit it!"

"That look was me giving God a piece of my mind," I said.

"Good place to encounter God, here in the land of Gitche Manitou."

"Can we go somewhere less spiritual next year? Somewhere with a pool and a bar and no God? I'm thinking Vegas."

"I'm thinking a sailing trip down the inland waterway to Chesapeake Bay. You'll love it. I watched you today. You're a natural."

"You always say that after you nearly kill me."

"Let's talk about it over drinks."

"Right," I said, and I took Bob's hand in mine.

Leslie Bamford is happy to be alive after sixteen years of marriage to her adventurous husband. Bob's idea of a good time usually involves some sort of death-defying experience. This makes for good stories later, written in the safety of her home with a quirky puppy named Merlin at her side and occasional visits from her mother's ghost. She gains a wry perspective on life through her writing. She has had several stories published in Summit Studios anthologies, including in Mugged by a Moose *(2006),* A Beaver is Eating my Canoe *(2008) and* Mob Hit on My Grandmother's Dog *(2014).*

Rite of Passage

In pursuit of Saskatchewan's notorious "slough shark."

By Cheryl Schenk

Every lake in cottage country echoes with the laughter of children and the sounds of summers past, as was the case in 1964 when my twelve-year-old brother Brian and eleven-year-old cousin Glen faced the first challenge on their journey to manhood.

Our family was on vacation at my aunt and uncle's cabin at Christopher Lake, just north of Prince Albert, Saskatchewan. It was a quiet place, with several cabins nestled between the pine, spruce, and poplar trees rising up from the lake's beaches. Christopher Lake was where we had learned to swim and water ski, and where we had became beachcombers and berry pickers. In late summer, our lips would turn a dark shade of purple as we picked and gorged ourselves on Saskatoon berries. We swam with the minnows, splashed in the water until our lips turned blue, and dodged horseflies that were always trying to separate us from a pound of flesh.

The boy's challenge was laid out around the campfire one night, when my father and two uncles teased them mercilessly about their lack of success while fishing. They suggested that the noisy boys had scared all the fish into the lake's darkest depths. At first the boys had taken the ribbing with good humor, but soon they had reached their limit and decided to come up with a plan.

"Tomorrow morning we're gonna catch the biggest fish in the lake," Brian told the adults.

Ignoring the boisterous laughter, Glen backed him up. "We'll show you," he said.

Truth be known, they didn't have much of a plan. But one thing they did have was plenty of determination.

The following morning the boys got up before anyone else, including the sun. With fishing poles and tackle boxes in hand, they made their way through the trees toward a rickety set of wooden steps that led them down to the lake. They were on a mission; their impending manhood was at stake.

They made their way to the end of the pier, where a small log raft was moored. They loaded their gear and donned a pair of ugly orange life vests, which they knew to wear at all times. This was one of my uncle's rules. Grabbing the paddles, they pushed away from shore and moved to where the water deepened.

By the time the boys had found their perfect fishing spot and settled in, the sun had poked its flaming head above the eastern shore. They baited their hooks with minnows, dropped their lines, and sat back smugly as they waited for the fish to bite.

Up to that point, they had been fairly quiet—or as quiet as young boys are apt to be. As sunbeams spread across the lake, warming the cold morning air, they tried very hard not to make any sound.

It wasn't long before one of the lines had a bite. The fish tugged hard, bringing both boys to rapt attention. They worked excitedly—one of them playing the jackfish with the rod while the other prepared to pull the fish onto the raft. Somehow they managed to coax the fish on board. It was only then that the boys realized, with some dismay, that a northern pike does not lie down and die willingly, even when it's out of the water.

As the fish flopped around on the raft, the boys tried to prevent its escape while at the same time keeping their fingers away from its flapping jaws. Their fathers referred to the jackfish as a "slough shark" because of its dozens of sharp, needle-like teeth.

The raft was flat and had no sideboards. Moreover, the boys had neglected to bring a net, which meant that to dispatch the fish they had to use their paddles. As they began swinging wildly at the fish, trying to connect with its head, the jackfish was only alarmed further. The scene became a dance to the death.

For a time, during the ensuing drama, it was probably not obvious who was more terrified: the fish or the boys. Paddles and teeth lashed out, but in the end the fish was no match. Unfortunately, it had been beaten beyond recognition.

Regaining their composure, the boys coaxed the raft back toward the pier. The entire clan and half of the extended community were there to greet them—all had been aroused by the commotion on the water and had witnessed most of it from shore.

So it was, at Christopher Lake on a summer morning in 1964, that my brother and cousin confronted their fears and came home with a large jackfish. They beamed proudly as they waded to shore, where they presented the pathetic pulp that was their fish to my aunt.

"When do we eat?" they asked.

Cheryl Schenk has traveled from cottage country to any backwater coffee shop that will allow her to sit with her muse while compiling the next story. She is the independently published author of a children's book titled Little Synni's Moonlight Mischief. *Her sporadic blog can be found at* **www.bittleberry.blogspot.ca**.

Crocs

You have what *inside that barn?*

By Alex Hamilton-Brown

Toronto can be like a sweat lodge in August, and one memorable Monday morning in 1998 was no exception.

The temperature was already in the mid-eighties when I climbed the wooden stairs to my office on the third floor of the old brownstone building in Toronto's Downtown Eastside. I had just opened a window to let some air inside when the phone rang. I picked up and heard the thick accent of Yuri Voronov, a Russian freelance cameraman with whom I had produced a couple of documentaries for the National Film Board of Canada. Yuri's camera work was excellent, even if his English took a bit of getting used to. He had come from Moscow to Toronto in 1995 and we had become good friends.

"Hi Yuri, you're back," I said. "How did things go in Jamaica?"

"You know, I shoot pilot film about crocodiles," he replied.

"You did?"

"Yes. Everything okay with filming, but now owners of croc farm have problem. They ship twelve crocodiles to Quebec zoo, but zoo can't take them for two more weeks. Now they are stuck at Toronto airport. They are in crates and suffer from heat. If we do not get them out of there, Al, they will die."

I wasn't sure what he meant by "we," so I blurted the first thing that came to my mind. "Maybe the Humane Society can take them."

"I think that would give big problem," said Yuri. "Humane Society only take domestic pets. Imagine small dogs and cats in same area as ten-foot crocodiles?"

I had to admit the image was not pretty—to say the least.

"Crocs have Red Robson with them," Yuri continued. "He is expert. His job is to take care of them. The Quebec zoo will pay all expenses if we can find place to keep them for a couple of weeks."

"What does this have to do with me?"

"Al, you have barn on your property up north, don't you?"

Straightaway, I realized where this was going.

"You're not seriously suggesting that we should bring the crocs to my cottage, are you?"

"Why not?" replied Yuri. "It's quiet up there. You have big barn, no?"

My property had a large log barn on it, built by the people who settled the Hastings Highlands in the mid-nineteenth century. It had been empty since I purchased the acreage in 1980. But the idea of turning it into a crocodile hideaway was bordering on crazy. I was in the business of filmmaking, not animal rescue. On the other hand, it was clear that Yuri was very worried about the fate of these creatures.

I told him to meet me at the Cherry Street diner in an hour. "We'll try to sort it out," I said. I wasn't exactly sure how we *could* sort it out, but we were good friends, so I said it anyway.

Yuri was already sitting at a window seat in the diner when I arrived. Even after filming under the Jamaican sun for two weeks, he hadn't picked up much of a tan. Yuri was of Russian-Mongolian descent. He was a wiry five-foot-six and his small eyes shone like black pearls as he described how Red Robson—a former stuntman—might wrestle with one of the eight-foot crocs in a pond on my property. Clinging to its back, Red could apparently spin the creature around in the water, making it look like a ferocious fight. Yuri produced a brochure that showed Red and his partner lassoing a huge crocodile, with tourists gawking from behind a high fence.

When coffee arrived, our conversation turned to the plight of the crocs at the airport.

"What about the Toronto Zoo?" I asked, "Surely they can help you out."

"Already tried," replied Yuri. "They told Red they have no room for them."

He leaned toward me. "Al, have you thought about farm? Red would be with them day and night."

I had thought about it. If I played host to twelve crocodiles in Ontario's cottage country, I'd need to buy extra insurance. I'd also need to have my head examined.

Yuri looked exasperated. "Hmmph," he muttered, exhaling through his nose. "Bloody Quebec Zoo. So unprofessional." He suddenly brightened. "Look, why don't we meet with Red at airport Hilton this afternoon? He will bring all documents for you to see. How about that?"

"Well, I suppose I could talk to him," I said. But I still had misgivings.

*   *   *

The croc wrangler known as Red Robson was a tall, powerful-looking man with short-cropped orange hair. He looked to be in his early thirties. He had a cheerful smile and spoke with a deep Texas drawl.

The import license and insurance papers he showed me were surprisingly comprehensive. They actually included stopover contingencies, exonerating all third parties. Clearly, whoever wrote it up had covered all the bases. This satisfied me that life, limb and property were at least covered.

"Al, do you have any idea what the floor area of your barn might be?" asked Red.

I tried to visualize the interior. "I'd say it's about fifteen by twenty-five feet," I replied. "And it has one window."

"How many doors?"

"Two. One at the front and one at the side. Both are padlocked."

"If y'all agree to help, I'll bring the crocs there at night in an unmarked truck. I'd just need you boys to help me unload the crates."

Parrying for a moment, I asked, "What about food?" I doubted there would be much in Bancroft for the crocs to eat.

"Oh they don't need no food," replied Red. "Crocodiles have a real slow metabolism. They can live for weeks without food."

I looked at Yuri, then back at Red. "Why not," I said, shrugging, "Let's do it."

The three of us left the Toronto airport at eleven o'clock that night. Yuri and I led the way in my car. Red followed in an unmarked rented truck, with his twelve crates of crocodiles stuffed inside. Three hours later, we were rumbling along the forest road leading to my property. It was a clear night and a full moon danced behind the poplar trees as we passed our little lake, casting shifting shadows across the calm water.

We reached the farm just after two a.m. When I saw the white truck silhouetted against the black barn, I had a sudden twinge of disquiet. Was I doing the right thing? Suppose one of the reptiles escaped into the lake? I could only imagine the headline in *The Bancroft Times*: MONSTER SIGHTED IN L'AMABLE LAKE. BANCROFT O.P.P. INVESTIGATING.

But it was too late for thoughts like that. By three a.m. all the crates were unloaded into the barn, and by four Red had the crocs lying at various angles on the wooden floor, their massive jaws bound with wire and burlap.

When Red came to unload the last crate, he let out a long, drawn-out whistle—a pregnant female had laid a clutch of eight eggs inside the crate. Normally, crocodiles lay their eggs in a depression in the sand and cover them until they hatch, but apparently this lady couldn't wait and had to make do with the crate.

Red took the eggs into the farmhouse and wrapped them lightly in a thick warm blanket. Soon after that we were sound asleep in our bunk beds.

After breakfast, Yuri and I watched as Red sprinkled water on the backs of the crocodiles to keep them moist and cool. With watering can in hand, he came up to a large crocodile lying in one corner of the barn. Suddenly, Red jumped back as the croc swung round, its massive jaws wide open.

"Whoa there, Mugger!" he hollered. Holding the watering can in front of him, he slowly backed away and joined us at the door. "Mugger must'a somehow worked the wire off his muzzle," he said.

"What you going to do?" asked Yuri.

"Oh, it's alright," said Red. "I got somethin' here in my pack that'll put him out for a bit." He took out a tranquilizing gun and loaded it. "This'll fix 'im for a while. You don't take chances with a croc like Mugger. He could have your arm off in seconds."

We nodded apprehensively.

Red shot a needle into Mugger's side, and within five minutes the creature had closed its mouth and was apparently asleep. Then, moving in from behind the croc, he re-tied the muzzle with wire and burlap.

After that episode, Yuri and I said our farewells to Red and returned to Toronto.

Because of filming commitments, it was ten days before the two of us got back to my property. This time, I brought my two children—ten-year-old Adam and eight-year-old Louise. As soon as we arrived, Adam had to use the washroom. He hurried from the car into the house. Twenty seconds later he bounded out again, crying in alarm. "Dad," he shouted. "There are crocodiles in the bath!" He had just finished peeing when he'd heard a high-pitched squawking sound. That's when he turned around and saw three baby crocodiles splashing in the shallow water of my bathtub.

"Oh yeah," said Red, in his usual laidback way. "The little guys hatched four days ago."

Louise squealed with delight when he showed her how to pick up the tiny reptiles without getting nipped.

"So, how have things been while we were away?" I asked.

"Jis' fine," he replied. "Oh, one thing. While you were away I had a couple of visitors. One mornin' last week, I had jis' finished boardin' up the window and front door of the barn when a face peers round the side door. It was a young kid. Said his name was Ray."

"That would be Ray Schlinger," I said. Ray was a sixteen-year-old from a neighboring chicken farm. He could be a nosy lad, almost to the point of harassment.

Red continued. "The kid stood at the doorway of the barn, bendin' his neck and tryin' to adjust his eyes to the darkness. He figured I had brought a load of chickens. He was tryin' to edge around me when I closed and padlocked the door."

Red smiled as he recalled what happened next. "I figured I'd stop him in his tracks from snooping around again, so I says to him, "I'm gonna level with you, son. I'm keepin' a few bodies in there. But, hey, they'll be gone in a few days.""

"He looked at me and his mouth dropped open. Then he gives me this scared-lookin' smile and skedaddles off real quick. That's the last I saw of anyone until the policeman showed up."

"What! The police have been here?" I gasped.

"Oh, it's OK," said Red. "It was just one officer. His name was P.C. Taylor. Said he was just followin' up on some cockamamie story about there bein' dead bodies in a barn."

"What did you tell him?" I asked. I wasn't sure I wanted to know.

"Well, I figured the best way was the straight way. So I said to him: 'Officer, I would like you to see inside the barn for yourself. But before you do, take a look at this brochure.' We sat down on the porch and I explained about my farm in Jamaica and how the Quebec Zoo had let us down. I showed him the crocs in the barn and said to him, 'Officer, I'm going to have to ask you to respect a confidence here. These are rare and dangerous animals. If the village folk were to know there are crocodiles here, this place would become a three-ring circus overnight. Can I ask you to treat this as confidential?' He said he could probably do that. But then he wasn't sure what to put in his notebook. So I told him, 'How about you just say that you noted there were some rare species of animals in the barn. These were bein' well cared for by their handler. By the end of the week, they will be en route to the Quebec Zoo. How does that sound?'"

Officer Taylor had taken down Red's suggestion almost word for word. Red smiled as he told us the last thing the policeman said to him before he drove off.

"I suppose you've guessed it was young Ray who filed the complaint?"

Red had nodded and the cop just shook his head.

"It makes me laugh to think of Ray talking about a bad smell comin' from the barn. Talk about bad smell. If there's one smell I can't stand around here, it's that stink comin' from them two thousand chickens on his folks' farm. I near choke to death every time I drive past there."

And that was the last Red had heard from the police, or anyone else for that matter. Later that day Red had phoned the Quebec Zoo and had been told that they were ready to receive the crocodiles.

From the batch of eight eggs, only three hatched. And as Red drove off they were squawking noisily at him from a basin on the passenger's seat.

They have a saying in Hastings Highlands. All guests make us happy: some by coming, and some by going. Red was a great guy, but I must admit I was happy to see his truck and his crocodiles heading down the highway toward Quebec.

Alex Hamilton-Brown is a Scottish Canadian writer and filmmaker whose work has managed to slip through various film festival cracks to win 25 international awards, including Giants: The Mystery and the Myth—*one of the Discovery Channel's most highly rated shows. In 2005 he received a $30,000 grant from the Canada Council for the Arts for an original ballet scenario, which was filmed in Paris for the CBC and starred Karen Kain. A dreamer, as well as a doer, Hamilton-Brown's award-winning poetry has been published in various North American anthologies— including* Milkweed Birds—*which received rave reviews from the Ontario Poetry Society. You can reach Hamilton-Brown at* **ahambro@sympatico.ca**.

Les Misérables and Marshmallows

Another way to search for the meaning of life.

By Pamela Patchet

When our children were young, we didn't have much money for summer vacations. Renting a villa in Italy would have to wait, and Disneyland in July didn't hold any appeal. Since our options were few, we decided one summer to try camping. Rather, my husband decided to try camping. I had to be convinced.

I never camped as a child. My husband, on the other hand, comes from a long line of outdoor enthusiasts. His father is a geologist who has spent years poking around in the bush with aboriginal guides. His grandfather was a first mate aboard a passenger vessel that traveled between Britain and Hong Kong, and his great-grandfather was a ship's captain who sailed around Cape Hope to go to the Klondike. Outdoor survival may be entrenched in my husband's genes, but my genes are firmly rooted in snug cafés that serve eggs Benedict and mimosas.

After my weak protests about bugs, sleeping on the ground, and bugs, I admitted defeat and began to research so that I could at least go into the experience prepared. I interrogated experienced campers, borrowed their equipment, and bought ingredients for s'mores. Undaunted by repeated references to "real challenge" when camping with children, I armed myself with Deep Woods

Off! and ignored suggestions that I should purchase a snakebite kit. We chose a lake that seemed far enough away to be an adventure, but close enough so that we could come home if necessary. With a new tent, sleeping bags, and coolers—both Styrofoam and alcoholic varieties—we embarked.

The first thing our kids noticed was the star-studded sky. They stood in awe, mouths hanging open at the vast black universe, and inhaled sweet wood smoke as they gazed out at the infinite panoply of the Milky Way.

The second thing they noticed was the open pit toilet. They stood in awe, mouths hanging open over the vast black hole, and inhaled pungent effluent as they gaped at what seemed to be infinite numbers of crawling spiders.

We soon realized the term "six man tent" (at least the one we purchased) is an egregious misnomer. Its manufacturers were either delusional or they tested the tent's capacity with grossly malnourished dwarves. Nevertheless, we had no choice but to squeeze inside and giggle our way to sleep.

We fell into a rhythm each day and learned to work as a team. My husband prepared breakfast and chopped wood for the evening campfire, while I prepared lunch and dinner and doled out snacks. Kids cheerfully hauled drinking water and washed the dishes in plastic tubs, playing at their own version of Survivor. We cooked with gas—well, propane, actually. And as for the adage "food tastes better outside"? Well, yes, in a manner of speaking it does. But by the time we typically got our fire going, dug the hot dogs out of the bottom of the cooler, threaded them onto sticks and cooked them, we would have happily eaten barbecued shoe leather and said it tasted good. Meals improved with experience and the help of a local store that supplied homemade pies and popsicles.

We all learned to slow down and absorb our surroundings. We watched in amazement one day as an eagle dove into the lake and flew off with a fish clutched in her talons. One early morning on the beach, we stumbled across a turtle that was methodically digging a hole, presumably for her eggs.

"This is better than TV," proclaimed my son with quiet conviction.

After a day of hiking and swimming in the lake, we would often paddle a canoe at sunset with our three children seated between us like a row of ducklings. Then, back at shore, we'd scamper around to prepare the bonfire before darkness cloaked the site. Sitting around that fire we'd sing all the classics: Kumbaya, Land of the Silver Birch, and Monty Python's Lumberjack Song. Ghost tales and stories about our children as babies were shared from memory, and though they'd heard them all before, the repetition was as soothing to them as the practiced prayers of church.

My husband brought Victor Hugo's classic *Les Misérables* to our little campsite. Every night, as we huddled between the folds of our blankets, he would share a bit more of the story of Jean Valjean and his nemesis Inspector Javert. The kids were captivated by the book's powerful message of redemption and compassion, and each night they'd beg for more.

By the end of our vacation, my husband finally finished the story. My little one paused in her quest for the perfect roasted marshmallow.

"So Dad," she began. "This story means sometimes that a bad man is really a good man, and sometimes a good man is really a bad man. And you have to look hard to see who is who, but if you look in their hearts and watch what they do, you'll just know. Right?"

As I smiled over her head at my husband, I knew that my café days were over.

Pamela Patchet is a former ad executive turned freelance writer. Now a cottage owner, she has happily said goodbye to tents, open-fire cooking, and pit toilets on rainy nights. As a writer, she attempts to expose her foibles to illustrate a larger truth. Luckily, exposing one's foibles in public is not a punishable offense. Her work has appeared in several anthologies, The Globe and Mail, The National Post, *and* The Montreal Gazette. *She also writes a regular column for* Watershed *Magazine. You can visit her at* **www.anovelwoman.blogspot.com**.

Swimming to Johnny Depp

Are you waving to me, my love?

By Katherine Fawcett

The nattering voices of children digging for snacks and towels and swim goggles; the incessant wheeze of a debarked wiener dog tied to a nearby picnic table; the shrieks of bikinied teenagers on inner tubes splashing each other.

It all faded to a dull hum when I saw Him.

Far across the rippling water, standing godlike on a raft in the middle of the lake, he looked untouchable. I shook my head and rubbed my eyes. Was it a mirage? A miracle? Heatstroke? He ran his fingers through his hair and wiped the back of his hand across his forehead. He shifted his weight from one hip to the other and licked his lips.

I heard birds singing. Exotic birds. Extinct exotic birds. And some harp music.

The distance between us was an eternity, and yet it was nothing. His body glistened in the sunlight—tanned and dripping wet. He had the sleek muscles and taut skin of a race horse. I didn't need my glasses to know that it was Johnny Depp. Without that French girl. I could see a Tibetan Mastiff by his side. He held a glass of chardonnay in one hand, a strawberry in the other. His hair curled down to his shoulders; they were the shoulders of a man who could hold me tenderly one moment and build a set of shelves the next—shelves for his collection of literary classics and tastefully framed photos of his mother.

Did I mention that he was naked as a peach? Oh yes, my friend. I squinted to see his nipples, pink as eraser heads.

What's that? Who ... me?

He motioned with his hand. I looked behind me, then back over the water toward him. He was pointing at me, gesturing with his finger. His gaze pierced my soul. I completely forgot that I was holding a half-peeled hardboiled egg in one hand. Warm liquid squirted through the straw of the juice box that I unconsciously squeezed with the other.

Understanding washed over me like syrup over a pancake. He wanted me to join him on the raft.

"Come alone," he whispered. The wind carried his words to me. I was sure of it.

Mom! Mom! Where's my boogie board? Mom! Petey's hogging the boogie board! Mom! Mom! Lexi ate all the chips! Don't push! He's pushing me! Hey! That was my egg!

It's staggering how much a person can block out when the love of one's life is beckoning from across a mountain lake. Truly staggering.

I stepped out of my Birkenstocks, pointed my arms over my head and dove into the lake—forgetting in the process that I don't know how to dive. My belly, triceps and thighs hit the water simultaneously with an ear-splitting *thwack!* But I was unfazed. In fact, the burning sensation made me feel alive.

I grabbed the ladder momentarily to catch my breath.

Mom? Mom? Are you okay? You've got all your clothes on. Petey—look! Mom's in the water with all her clothes on!

My senses were keen, my lungs fully oxygenated. I felt like I was forty again. I slipped my hairband off and tilted my head back toward the sun.

I would swim! I would swim to my love!

"Yes!" I sang out, exhilarated, shaking my hair in the cool, clear water. If I had been paying attention, I would have seen teenagers hanging silently from their inner tubes; the wiener dog with a flip-flop in his mouth; an egg bobbing in the water beside me.

"I'm coming, my love!" This mermaid was a long way from Saskatchewan.

I bent my knees and got ready to push away from the dock. I felt as sleek as a trout. No ... a dolphin!

But wait. From the water I could see him more clearly than ever. Johnny is an impatient man. He signaled for me to undress. "Down to your skivvies," he whispered on the wind.

I was a woman hypnotized. With one elbow wrapped around the ladder, I undid the belt and took off my cargo shorts underwater. I twirled them overhead and tossed them onto the dock. They landed with a *thaack!* and I was vaguely aware that my keys, my cell phone, my prescription drug refill, my bank card, some bug spray, and a pack of Clorets were still in the pockets.

I pulled my tank top off seductively. And my socks. The cool water against my underwear felt invigorating. I looked down and noticed that I was wearing an old maternity bra. It meant nothing to me. I knew that Johnny Depp wouldn't care. We had a deeper connection.

I pushed myself away from the dock and into the lake. My body, propelled with a sense of urgency, shot forward. Front crawl or breast stroke? I smiled knowingly, parting my arms in front of my body like the petals of a flower blossoming in the sun. I closed my eyes and experienced complete immersion.

They told me later that it was a good thing I had such a sturdy bra on. It gave the Newfie something to clamp his teeth on when he pulled me to shore.

"I swear to God, lady, you were blue."

"It was freaky."

"Yeah. And the weeds that came out of your mouth? Holy crap."

"I've never seen anything sink so fast!"

Someone found my glasses under the dock that afternoon. One arm was broken off, but they were otherwise fine. The swimmers' itch only lasted a few days. The kids refused to go back to the lake with me for the rest of the summer.

Johnny Depp must have returned to the south of France, and I know that Tibetan Mastiffs get mistaken for Newfies on occasion. In the meantime, I'm taking swim lessons at the pool. My instructor is this stocky, blond, blue-eyed Brad Pitt-type who seems to have a thing for older women.

Katherine Fawcett is a writer and musician who currently lives in Pemberton, BC. She fondly remembers summers at her family cottage on the shores of Lake Winnipeg, where she enjoyed burying her siblings in the sand. Her short fiction has appeared in numerous literary publications across Canada, including Event Magazine, subTerrain, Other Voices *and* Freefall. *She has been shortlisted by the CBC Literary Awards, won the Federation of BC Writers short fiction contest, and won* Event *Magazine's creative non-fiction contest. Her violin music has never won anything. In fact, she spent most of last summer digging the instrument out of a sand dune on the shores of Lake Winnipeg.*

Conjuring Lake Calamities

How to know if your best friend is trying to kill you.

By Sandra Jackson

There is a lovely little lake about an hour southwest of Edmonton named Wizard Lake. It sits in a long, narrow basin carved out by glaciers and is said to be extremely deep. Divers report that it appears to be bottomless in places; in others, it has house-sized boulders left behind when the glaciers receded.

The lake was originally called Conjuring Lake—another word for magic—and at sunrise on warm, misty mornings when the lake is perfectly still one can well imagine all kinds of mystical happenings. In the autumn, the leaves on the poplar trees surrounding Wizard Lake turn a bright yellow and are reflected across its surface. Water-skiing on such a day feels like skimming across a river of gold.

When I was growing up, Wizard Lake was my favorite place in the world. My parents purchased a parcel of land there in 1957, and the next summer—when I was eleven years old—we erected a small chalet-style cottage on a hill overlooking the water. We dubbed it the Shilly Chalet. Another family was building on the lot next to ours. As I was an only child, I was thrilled to discover that they had *five* children.

From a kid's perspective, Wizard Lake was a wonderfully safe place. There was no poison ivy, no dangerous snakes—just a beautiful treed landscape and a freshwater lake to play out our endless childhood ideas for discovery and adventure. There was really nothing that could go wrong in such an atmosphere.

Or was there?

The Ross's oldest son was a handsome, fun-loving boy named Jim. We were close in age and soon became fast friends. It didn't take me long to discover that he had a fertile mind for developing daring escapades … and they always seemed to include me.

It's a good thing I have a guardian angel, because as time went on I began to wonder if Jim—who appeared to be so nice—might actually be trying to do me in!

For example, inspired by Arthur Ransome's *Swallows and Amazons*, we decided to build a raft to get out onto the water. We imagined all the fun we would have pretending to be explorers or pirates. Since our fathers were clearing trees, we soon had enough logs to build an eight-by-eight-foot watercraft. As we nailed it together, we eagerly anticipated our many upcoming adventures.

The moment of truth arrived after we had pushed, pulled and dragged the beast down to the shoreline. I thought Jim was just being chivalrous when he insisted that I try the raft first. However, I soon discovered that fresh-cut green wood doesn't float very well; our "work of art" sank like a stone, leaving me soaking wet.

Thanks Jim!

As we got older, Jim and I developed an affinity for water sports—especially water skiing. Even though Jim had only water-skied twice before, he considered himself an expert. He had endless sage advice about how to get up into a standing position. A little more advice about how to stay up might have been helpful, too.

While I was attempting multiple times to "get up" behind the neighbor's ski boat, Jim stood on the shore shouting directions and encouragement. In doing this he was also drawing friendly neighborhood attention to the whole scene. About the time I finally managed to stay up, I had quite an audience, thanks to Jim. Unfortunately, my one-piece bathing suit chose that moment to break a supporting strap. It flopped down, leaving me uncovered from the waist up.

While I was pleased to finally be skimming across the water, as free as a bird, I was feeling a little freer than I had intended. To the sound of cheering, I let go of the rope and sank beneath the surface of the water, which did a splendid job of covering my red face.

I can still remember my father throwing a big towel over my head and hauling me unceremoniously into the boat.

Thanks Jim!

In time, we invented the rules for more water sports. One of our favorites was "time trials" in the family fishing boats. An ongoing topic of conversation was how to achieve more speed. Jim's family had a twelve-foot boat with a seven-and-a-half horsepower engine. It was a speedy little thing. Our family had a ten-foot boat with an eight horsepower motor. For the purposes of racing they were pretty evenly matched, and we spent many happy hours trying to "captain" the winning watercraft.

On one fateful day, we took our places at the imaginary starting line. We counted to three and then gunned our engines. The top speed we could achieve was probably around thirty kilometers per hour. In about twenty seconds we could get the boats to hydroplane, and another five seconds was required to reach top speed.

In less than a minute it became obvious that Jim was the winner, so I slowed to an idle. Jim pumped his fist in the air and laughed as he ran circles around me. All of a sudden, I realized that the arc he was cutting in the water was going to bring him a little too close to my boat. The look of glee on his face turned to horror. As he careened closer and closer he tried to bank the boat away from me, but to no avail.

With a sickening *crunch!* the gunwale of Jim's boat hit the back left corner of mine, which propelled me forward several meters and almost catapulted me into the water. Things became very quiet as we assessed the damage.

My boat, the Oz of Wizard, was a sturdy little wooden craft built by my father to withstand the tests of time and weather. It had approximately fifteen coats of fiberglass applied by my dad, which made it very durable. At the crash scene, I merely had to brush off a little bit of fiberglass powder. However, Jim's boat didn't fare quite so well—there was a two-inch gash in the side and he was taking on water. The worst part was having to explain all of this to his father.

As for me personally, I was bit traumatized by the event and had nightmares about flying boats for some time afterwards.

Thanks Jim!

The highlight of Jim's plot to off me started innocently enough. It was the May long weekend, and the Rosses had a city neighbor who had donated three cardboard boxes full of fireworks for our annual fireworks show. Thanks to our boat-racing debacle the previous summer, the Ross family had also purchased a larger and safer boat, which would be perfect for water skiing. We could hardly wait.

On the afternoon of the fireworks show, all of the Ross family except Jim had gone to the nearby country store. My parents were watering some small evergreens with pails of water from the lake. Jim and I were at loose ends, pondering what we could do to liven things up a little. History suggests that this is never a good state of mind for two youngsters given to mishap and mayhem.

For some reason, Jim and I decided that we should perform a test run. The plan was to light a few firecrackers from the dock so that when we threw them they would land harmlessly in the water. Predictably, one thing led to another, and to another, and to another. My last clear memory was of Jim standing in his cabin at the kitchen table—with a live sparkler in his hand—digging through three large boxes of fireworks looking for more blockbusters.

I was standing ten feet from the door when I began to notice a bright yellow shimmer erupting from one of the boxes. At almost the same moment, Jim recognized what had happened. Thankfully, he also realized the seriousness of the situation.

"Get out of the way!" he shouted.

Somehow he managed to grab all three of the boxes at once. He burst through the back door of his cottage and hurled them up the path toward the area where I had just tripped and fallen flat on my face. Was his master plan to off me about to succeed?

Rockets and pinwheels, blockbusters and fountains, all went off in one incredible bonanza of light and sound. It would have been an amazing display worthy of "grand finale" if we'd been in the mood for it. But at that moment, Jim and I were preoccupied with having to explain to his parents how the cottage had burned down.

Fortunately my parents, who had observed that something was amiss, came to the rescue with the pails of water they were carrying for the tree saplings. They quickly doused the inferno—and me—and put the fire out.

The Ross family chose that moment to return from their shopping trip. All of us stood speechless as we watched our dream fireworks show go up in flames.

Needless to say, we weren't allowed to go water skiing that weekend.

Thanks Jim!

After more than thirty years of fun at Wizard Lake, the Shilly Chalet was sold in 1989. Jim and Sandra have remained friends all these years. Most recently, on a trip to visit Jim and his wife Patti Lee on Vancouver Island, they became lost while exploring the Gulf Islands in Jim's powerboat, Bad Dog.

Up to My Neck in Adventure

Sometimes the river gods demand sacrifice.

By Amy Attas

It was only after the river soaked my hair and swept my hat away that I realized I was in over my head. My legs were still in my kayak—which had flipped over and was bobbing in the rapids—but my torso was pinned against a rock shelf while my head craned above the undulating current. One hand gripped my paddle while the other was jammed against the river bottom, desperately trying to keep my nose in the air. And I waited there, in the most turbulent part of the rapids, for at least half a minute. I pondered my fate, my choices, my probability of death—incapable of doing anything but wait for the river to push the plot forward. Finally, the river's current pulled me from my boat and set me free.

Eighteen hours earlier I had been at a reunion breakfast with some high school friends. Between stories of our university experiences I had talked up my plans to kayak the Whitemouth River. Like everyone else who's never kayaked, they mentioned the fear of being stuck in an overturned boat and unable to reach air. I admitted that I didn't know how to roll a kayak, but that any time I had flipped I'd been able to slip right out—no training, no panic, no worries. Besides, after spending a cautious childhood on flat water I figured that it was time for some adventure.

I am one of those odd kids who actually grew up in cottage country—on the doorstep of Whiteshell Provincial Park near Pinawa, Manitoba—and for twenty years I'd taken it for granted. Sure, I had fond memories of jogging through the forest with only deer and black bears for company, skiing twenty kilometers from my back door on groomed trails, and diving into a lake of reflected stars on a clear summer's night. Most of the year the woods were quiet and the trails empty; cars stopped in the street while locals shouted to each other through their driver's side windows. The Loppet, the triathlon, golf season, and beach weather brought strangers to town—but mostly we ignored them. Yet through all of it, I had yearned for crowded streets and hipster cafés, loft apartments and grungy music clubs. Now that I'd experienced a bit of the wider world, I was eager to revisit cottage country and re-immerse myself in nature.

After my first year of university, I'd tried the Whitemouth River for the first time and had found a different sort of adventure. My guidebook had suggested paddling it in the springtime, before the river could dry to a trickle. Unfortunately, I hadn't been able to find the time to go until mid-July.

Two minutes into that initial trip and I was stuck—run aground in the middle of the parched streambed. I was forced to get out and push my boat into deeper water. Then it happened again. Over and over I was forced to climb out of my boat and drag it through the ankle-deep water. Sometimes I was able to hop in and paddle without hitting the river bottom, but often I was heaving myself over rapids like a child at the top of a toboggan run, thrusting the boat and myself forward one inch at a time.

I had passed Gary's Place, a gorgeous house carved into the granite where the local recluse spends his retirement. The only part of the river that was deep enough to float my kayak had been right next to a garden that Gary was busily weeding. I had tried to float past without disturbing his trance, but my paddle gurgled. Gary, with his long silver hair and hemp pants the color of rose quartz, had turned slowly and welcomed me like an old friend he was expecting for tea. In the time it took me to float from earshot, he was able to give me advice on shooting the next set of rapids and wished me luck finding deep water in summer's heat. Some recluse.

The next landmark had been a large house with a green lawn sloping down to the largest rapids on the river. The guidebook referred to them as Nevas Falls, but in the heat of summer it was barely Nevas Faucet. The water had been moving so slowly that I was able to float up to the drop-off, choose a path, then paddle backward and take a run. Two kids had sprinted out of the house and down the lawn to watch my attempt. I felt the weight of those who had gone before me, like Atreyu in *The Neverending Story* trying to pass between the gaze of two golden statues before they sensed his fear. I had no fear, and though it was more challenging than I had expected, I made it through just fine.

Eight months later I was back on the river, this time in the middle of a very wet spring. Young trees were submerged up to their crowns along the river's swollen banks, and my mother's well-wishing words were swept away as I shot beneath the Elma bridge. I made it to Gary's in ten minutes instead of half an hour, but was too busy charting a safe course to drop in for tea. I was drifting faster than a runner on shore, even without paddling. The next time I looked up, the house with the sloping lawn was rising up before me. I realized then that I was hurtling toward Nevas Falls.

There was no time to think about portages or ducking into a back eddy. I reminded myself that this was what I wanted—adventure, challenge, a wild experience. I assumed that I would be fine as long as I kept paddling.

I was wrong.

Suddenly I was up to my neck in rapids, thinking about the kayak lessons that would have been a good investment. The water surged and pulled me from the boat, then down into the depths and back to the surface again. Like a good captain I tried to stay with my kayak—one hand on the cockpit and the other on my paddle. But the river pulled me under again, which ripped the boat from my hand.

I tumbled through the murky water, unsure of where the rocks, the shore, or even the sky was. It was like being inside a washing machine during its spin cycle. I put trust in my life jacket, which up to that point had never failed to find its way to the surface.

A few moments later I was able to gasp for air. I was alive—for the moment—but I couldn't see my boat. Was it lost to the river? I cursed myself for not putting two hands on it. I should have dropped the paddle and stayed with the boat. A paddle was fifty dollars to replace; my kayak was worth seven hundred.

I struggled to claw my way to shore as my clothes and kayak skirt created significant drag. I gripped my paddle with one hand, while in the other I clutched the rubber tubing that had been lining my kayak's cockpit. Once I had reached the shoreline, I waded between the drowning aspens and crawled up onto that sprawling green lawn.

I gazed at the falls while I caught my breath and tended to my elbow, which was bleeding. I caught glimpses of red as my kayak bobbed in the whitewater, churning between the standing waves. If it stayed there, would I be able to retrieve it? I waded back into the current, but even before I was up to my knees I turned back. The current was too strong. I was too tired. There was no way.

I climbed the lawn to the house and rang the doorbell. A small boy answered, and when I explained my situation, he handed me a phone. My mother was not reachable—waiting to pick me up downstream—so I called my father at work. It was a humbling experience for an adventurer who thought she was autonomous.

My dad assured me that he would drive out on his lunch break. When I gave the phone back, I asked the boy's mother how often she received waterlogged wayfarers, seeing as how they lived at the most challenging point on the river. She said this was actually the first time—usually people weren't silly enough to paddle alone.

Later that afternoon, when I was safely back at home, I sat down with some hot chocolate and tried to forget the day's events. They seemed more horrifying in memory than they had been to live firsthand. My parents were keen to return to the river and attempt to locate the kayak. I told them it couldn't be done. They suggested we take the canoe and all the rope in the house, but I didn't want to go back. I'd had enough adventure for one day. I would save my money and buy a new kayak ... after my pride had been restored. I figured I should leave that one as a token payment to the river gods.

But my parents were thirsting for adventure. The thought of plucking a kayak from the froth of Nevis Falls—assuming that it was still there—was too exciting for them to pass up. So they persuaded me to get in the van.

I was tense for the entire drive. We traveled west for twenty minutes to escape Pinawa, which is nestled on the slow-moving Whiteshell River. Then we turned south, and planned to drive along the Whitemouth River until we reached Nevis Falls. I tried to emphasize the futility of our mission, but my parents' spirits would not be dampened. When we reached the town of Whitemouth I fell silent. This was where my mother had been waiting to pick me up—the planned endpoint of the day's adventure. The fact that I hadn't made it there in my kayak brought back the feeling of shame.

My mother suddenly stepped on the brakes. She pointed. Coming at us from the opposite direction were two teenagers on ATVs. The first had no cargo, but the second had a kayak strapped to the back. A red kayak. *My* kayak.

We made a U-turn and chased them back through town: a blue minivan carrying a canoe in hot pursuit of two ATVs with a kayak. It ended in the driveway of a house, and we spilled out of the van so that I could tell them my story. I emphasized the despair of my loss—the kayak was, in fact, a prized birthday present. They then told us their story, emphasizing the work they'd done to pluck it from the river. They had found it pinned to a nearby bridge and had spent hours bailing out water before they could drag it ashore. We all marveled at the distance the boat had traveled on its own, likely along the river bottom for part of the way, judging by its many new scrapes.

I was stunned by our luck. Had we been five minutes earlier or five minutes later, I would never have seen it again.

I offered the kids forty bucks. They grudgingly accepted. Then we stuffed the kayak into the back of our van and drove away before they could change their minds.

Amy Attas is a graduate of York University's Creative Writing program. Her stories have appeared in anthologies by Summit Studios and Cumulus Press, and her reviews have been published in The Rover *and* The Winnipeg Review. *She grew up in Pinawa, Manitoba, and now lives wherever there are trees to be planted.*

Camp Thief

The guilty will eventually be proven innocent.

By Lori-Lee Bott

During the 1970s, our family would set up a camp on Kennedy Lake every summer, which is nestled in the forested hills of Vancouver Island between Ucluelet and Port Alberni. As soon as school was over, it was time to scout for a secluded camping area that would offer some privacy. Once found, my parents would pack up the family and settle us in to what would be our temporary home until Labor Day.

To help out around the campsite, my mother always invited one of our older cousins to stay with us. Over the course of the summer, we would often have several cousins as well as family friends staying with us at the camp. We were rarely alone.

When we arrived at the boat launch, we would load up as much gear as would fit in our sixteen-foot boat, leaving just enough space for two people. As the trip from dock to camp was often more than an hour, my dad would take our mom first so that she could begin setting everything up before he returned for us. Several trips were often needed to carry all the gear and children, which meant it was an all-day event. The last of us usually didn't arrive at camp until dusk. Looking back, I don't know how they did it, but as an adult I can now understand why we stayed all summer.

On weekends, other family members would arrive. We would play on the beach, sunbathe, explore the forest, and swim in the lake. Sometimes my parents would go out in the boat for a few hours to explore or to search for great new fishing spots. They would leave us behind with one of our older cousins in charge.

As far as camp goes, our routine was to pitch our massive orange and blue canvas tent at the tree line, and then store all the coolers and boxes of dry goods behind it. Among other things, we set up a kitchen area with camp chairs, a large table, and a propane cookstove. This is where much of the action took place.

Breakfast was cereal and fruit, while lunch was usually sandwiches. Dinner was only slightly fancier: it typically consisted of wieners and beans, chili, burgers, baked potatoes or fresh-caught trout. We were not allowed to help ourselves to food without permission, and snacking between meals was a rarity. The treats would be handed out when my mom decided to hand them out. We had to carefully ration what we had.

One day, after our mom returned from boating, she was upset that somebody had taken a few of my father's cookies. She spoke to each of us, and every one in turn proclaimed his or her innocence. This made her really upset because one of us had to be lying. She gave us a stern lecture about not telling the truth and about taking food without permission. We all stuck to our stories, however, which clearly frustrated her.

Unfortunately, as the days passed, my father's cookies continued to go missing. Worse, all of us continued to claim we were innocent.

Looking back, I'm not surprised that my mother was upset. We were living on a remote beach with no easy access to a grocery store. She knew that one of us had to be lying. We didn't have a dog with us to blame; not that a dog could have opened a bag of cookies without tearing it to shreds.

We started to spy on each other. I don't remember whose idea it was, but my brother and I decided to hide behind our tent to try and catch the culprit. We laid our beach towels down and spent the day intently watching the cookie box. We were tired of being blamed for something we hadn't done.

Eventually our little plan worked—sort of. As we watched with rapt attention, a mink stole out of the forest and approached the bag of cookies. Daintily, he used his tiny paws to open the package, then took a cookie between his tiny jaws and disappeared back into the forest. My brother and I could hardly believe our eyes!

When my mother returned we told her what had happened. This made her even angrier, because she assumed we had concocted a fantastical story to protect our own guilt. We pleaded with her to believe us and finally convinced her to take a few minutes to sit down quietly by the tree and watch.

Our luck turned. The mink came back to the crime scene, opened the bag of cookies, and disappeared with another one in his teeth. We followed him for a short distance, noticing that he left a trail of cookie crumbs that led into the dense brush.

Mom apologized to all of us, and to show that she meant it we were allowed to share what was left of the cookies. By that time it was mostly crumbs!

Lori-Lee Bott was raised in a small "Wet Coast" town on Vancouver Island, close to nature, animals, camping, hiking, and boating. Lori-Lee and her family moved to the Kootenays and continue to explore the outdoors at every opportunity.

Living in Cottage Country

Sometimes the dream doesn't equal the reality.

By Paul Feist

Cottage country has a visceral appeal for many Canadians. It can be argued that a weekend at the cottage for some swimming, boating, fishing, or simply lazing on the dock with one's favorite book or libation is the quintessential Canadian experience during the summer months.

It's an entirely *different* experience when you live and work in cottage country. My wife Janice and I moved to the Muskokas in 1987 to operate the Port Sandfield Marketeria—a general store on Lake Rosseau. We knew we were fortunate, because all of our city friends kept telling us how lucky we were. Gazing across the lake from our living room, we thought we had died and gone to heaven. We were also excited that we lived only twenty paces from where we worked. This short commute—compared to the endless wasted hours of sitting in traffic on Toronto's freeways—made us giddy at the thought of an extra hour or two of sleep every morning.

At some point during the May long weekend, we realized that our dream of sleeping in was pure fiction. Our daily routine now consisted of providing milk, bread, meat, and ice cream to all the cottage goers who were there on vacation, and we had to get up by six thirty so that we could open shop at eight. Twice per week I had to get up at four a.m. to greet the milkman. Those mornings I usually stayed up to cut meat for the display counter and to make sure our bakery—which was baked fresh every morning by a mildly eccentric woman who had the bad habit of burning herself frequently—was up and rising. We also had a staff of twelve students whose idiosyncrasies, at times, turned our dreams into nightmares.

We eventually realized the twelve-hour days were taking a toll on us physically and mentally, and that we needed a break. We decided that after the Labor Day weekend we would close the store for three days during midweek.

Since opening the store in May, we had managed to make friends with many of our regular customers. One of them graciously offered an empty cottage for our planned three-day mini-vacation. The hectic holiday Monday finally came to a close, leaving us completely exhausted. Nevertheless, on Tuesday morning Janice packed the car with food, wine, books, and bathing suits. Our Australian shepherd, Sheba, and all her doggie paraphernalia were the last items to get loaded inside.

I was surprised at how much there was to do before leaving, to the point where I began wondering if it was more trouble than it was worth. Each cooler and freezer had to be checked to make sure the temperatures were correct. The vegetables had to be taken from the display case and lugged into the walk-in cooler. All the fresh meat had to be wrapped in cellophane or vacuum-sealed to keep it fresh. The holiday weekend also meant that all my grocery orders had to be placed by Tuesday morning in order for us to receive them by early Friday.

Several times on the morning of our departure, I questioned whether we should even go to the cottage. Since our student staff had all returned to school, I suggested to Janice that we stay put and just relax around the house so that we could keep an eye on the store. Janice continued to calmly pack the car, which only increased my frustration level. I could feel my blood pressure rising.

"Enough is enough," Janice said, pulling me from my work. "The store will be here when we return."

It was only a short distance up to our utopian retreat. Unfortunately, my mind was still on store business as I climbed into the car and began driving. Janice sat beside me while Sheba lay in the back seat guarding a package of steaks.

From out of nowhere, three deer suddenly ran out of the woods and directly into our path. Despite my state of anxiety, I still had the reflexes to slam on the brakes. Janice began yelling, "UP! UP!" which I assumed was a signal to close the rear window to prevent Sheba from jumping out and chasing after the deer.

At almost the same instant I became aware of a car in my rearview mirror closing the distance fast.

A moment after that, Janice started shouting, "DOWN! DOWN!"

Distracted as I was, I naturally thought her "DOWN!" command was a signal for Sheba to lie down and be a good dog. But she shouted again and frantically pointed toward the back seat. A quick glance and I realized the dog's head was caught in the vice-like grip of the closing window.

I found myself in the peculiar position of watching the deer bound across the road in front of us, watching the car braking behind us, and at the same time frantically searching for the down button to free Sheba's head. Doors locked and various windows went up and down as I fumbled for the controls. The rear window finally began to lower, allowing an almost comatose Sheba to collapse on the seat, gasping for air. The deer disappeared and the irate driver behind me—unaware that our dog had nearly choked—roared past displaying the middle digit. I could only assume he was from out of town.

The entire chaotic episode took less than ten seconds.

We sat in silence for the rest of the journey as our jangled nerves settled and the dog's breathing slowly returned to normal. Sheba no longer showed interest in our steaks, which now lay strewn on the rear floor beside an assortment of cheese and wine.

When we arrived at the cottage we could see that it was beautiful and very secluded. We quietly unpacked and did our best to settle in. It was an unseasonably hot September afternoon, so we donned our bathing suits, prepared a couple of drinks, and went out onto the deck to unwind.

It wasn't long before the combination of peace, the sun's warmth, and a refreshing drink helped me forget about the store. I glanced over at my bride with great affection and thoughts of love. We had only been married for about six months and we hadn't yet had a honeymoon, so I suggested that I prepare another cocktail to go along with a nude sunbathing session. While I went inside, Janice arranged the chair cushions on the deck. Soon we were lying side by side, basking in the sun's warming rays and enjoying the serenity of our sanctuary. Amorous thoughts—the kind that had largely been neglected since we had opened the store—began percolating to the surface.

That was the last thought I remember before falling asleep.

Two hours later I woke with a start. I glanced over at my still-slumbering wife and instead saw a lobster. I tried to wake her gently.

"My God, look at you," she squeaked. "You're bright red."

"We've done it this time, babe," was all I could say.

We ached all over, but we managed to get up and escape into the cottage. Sheba, who had been sleeping inside, was excited to see us and began to jump up. She seemed hurt when I told her in no uncertain terms that we did *not* want to play.

We changed into some loose summer garments. I also managed to find some lotion, but applying it felt like dragging sandpaper over our skin.

Despite our severe burns, we figured that we would survive without going to the hospital. While sipping a Chardonnay, Janice asked what I wanted for dinner. We decided the steaks would have to wait, as merely saying the word "barbecue" made us feel like we were burning up. She suggested boiling some hot dogs, but given my condition the thought of a boiled wiener seemed inappropriate.

That night we slept on our backs with no touching allowed; even a goodnight kiss was out of the question, as our lips looked like we had both overindulged at the Botox clinic. Every time one of us tried to move it elicited a woeful groan from the other, which must have caused Sheba to wonder what was going on. For the rest of our stay we couldn't even hug each other.

The next day was cloudy and we were able to enjoy a short walk in the woods, though we had to be careful not to move too quickly. Even packing the car on our last day was a slow, painful, and delicate operation.

The store opened again on Friday morning. All of our grocery orders had come in, and the shelves were fully restocked and waiting for the usual onslaught of customers. As chance would have it, the friends who had loaned us their cottage were two of the first customers to arrive.

"You look great," said the man. "Nice tan. I hope you enjoyed yourselves. Did you manage to use the boat to do some fishing? And did you jump off the boathouse roof for fun, like we suggested?"

"No, we mostly just lay around in the sun," I replied, not wanting to go into details. "But we had a lot of fun. Thanks again for letting us use your cottage."

"It's our pleasure. Glad you had a good time."

"Now what can I get for you?"

"We're going to keep it simple tonight. Give me a package of those Red Hot wieners."

Paul Feist was mountain climbing in Tibet when he happened upon the "Deli Llama." He was so taken with their Llama on Rye that he continued trekking to the arts community of Muskoka, where he opened The Salvador Deli. After ten years of running his deli, he became deli-rious and began writing. When not writing, he spends time on stage as his alter ego Dorkin Barnes, a farmer of questionable IQ.

All is Well

It's all fun and games until somebody's cottage catches on fire.

By B.A. Markus

I hadn't planned to leave my husband while getting away from it all on Canada's West Coast. It just happened that way.

If I'd planned it, I certainly would have saved enough money so that I could have afforded to rent a place. Instead, the morning after the very difficult phone conversation in which I'd called it quits with my husband Lorne, I found myself three thousand miles from home on a small island that boasted breathtaking views of the mountains and sea. It also boasted what is probably the highest per capita compost-toilets-to-population ratio in Canada, and eight hundred of the quirkiest characters you'd ever hope to meet.

But there was no bank machine.

I had two hundred dollars in my pocket and a joint bank account with a man I'd just blown off after twelve years of marriage. A man who, as well as being a partner in one of the biggest corporate law firms in Toronto, would have no qualms about withdrawing every last penny from our bank account just to teach me a lesson.

It was obvious that I could no longer afford to stay at the bed-and-breakfast I'd originally booked for the duration of my month-long getaway. A little time alone had suddenly turned into a full-fledged flight from the confines of matrimonial misery, and for the first time in twelve years I had to fend for myself.

Like I said, I hadn't planned to leave my husband. But for some reason Green Island (not its real name) has that effect on people. You just never know what's going to happen when you board the ferry that takes you from the shores of Vancouver Island across the Georgia Strait to this tiny thirty-square-kilometer island. Fortunately, as crazy and unpredictable as life gets on Green, things always seem to work out. Which is why within an hour of realizing that I was effectively homeless and almost penniless, I saw the notice on the bulletin board at the library asking if somebody on the island was interested in a house-sitting gig.

I called the number from a phone booth outside the library and was invited right over.

Jeff and Paula and their two kids lived on a quiet stretch of gravel road that rolled and dipped, offering up fleeting views of the Coast Mountains on the faraway mainland. I made the typical city person mistake and went to the front door. Jeff came out the back and ushered me in that way, up the four wooden steps and through the mudroom.

It was a comfortable, ramshackle house that smelled like a combination of homemade bread, woodsmoke and old dog. Downstairs was a big cluttered kitchen with windows that looked out on the yard, and a living room amply stocked with worn-out couches and La-Z-Boy chairs. Books, magazines, cassette tapes, and CDs were piled everywhere. Upstairs, Jeff showed me the master bedroom and the kids' rooms, all of them bursting with the detritus of family life.

"Sleep wherever you want," he said apologetically. "Sorry about the mess."

We went back down the narrow, uneven stairs to the first floor.

"Ever use a woodstove?" Jeff asked.

"Sure." I was afraid Jeff would change his mind if he discovered how little I knew about country life in general and woodstoves in particular. But he must have suspected my lack of experience because he spent a long, long time explaining in great detail how the stove worked and showing me the woodpile and the kindling and the big red fire extinguisher on the wall.

Just as he was finishing up, Paula came in. She was less than five feet tall with delicate bones, but when she shook my hand I could feel the strength and resilience that ran through her like an electric current.

"Hi." She gave me a gentle smile. "Did Jeff tell you about the dog?"

Jeff hadn't mentioned the dog, although the smell I'd noticed when I stepped in the door had led me to suspect that there was one around.

"I like dogs," I said, hoping to endear myself further. "It'll be nice to have some company on my walks."

Paula laughed. "Don't count on it. Sasha hasn't made it down the drive in months." I followed my hosts into the mudroom. Curled up in a worn wicker doggie bed behind the freezer was the family pet, a barrel-chested black lab gone gray around the eyes and snout. The old dog lifted her head when we came in and opened her eyes, but it was obvious that she was totally blind from cataracts. I could tell she was friendly from the way she wagged her tail and from the little musical whimpering sounds she made.

"She smells bad, but she's a real good dog." Paula leaned down to pat Sasha on the head. "Aren't you, old girl?" Sasha wagged her tail again and whimpered.

"Her arthritis is worse with all this rain," Jeff explained. "If this keeps up, you might have to carry her down the back steps so she can go."

"That's okay. I'm sure I'll be fine." I leaned down to give Sasha a little pat.

"Great," Jeff said. "We're leaving on Monday."

The move from the bed-and-breakfast to Jeff and Paula's house was easy. They'd left the keys to their pickup and I didn't have much stuff—just a couple of boxes of books, my clothes, and my laptop.

After I had moved in, I made myself a cup of tea and took a couple of deep breaths to try and relax. It was time to call my mother and tell her about my breakup.

I flashed back thirteen years to the day I had called her from a campground on Cape Breton Island to tell her that I was engaged to Lorne and that we planned to get married the following summer. I was nineteen and my father had already been sick for five years. Even over the phone, I could feel her relief. Her youngest and wildest daughter would now be someone else's responsibility. Lorne had everything, and she didn't have to look after me anymore.

Now I had to tell her that we were getting a divorce.

"Hi Mom, it's Eve."

"Darling, where are you?" She always asked me that question when I called from Green, like she was hoping I had come to my senses and was calling her from my cell phone in the elevator of her condo building.

"Still here. On Green Island."

"I saw the weather on the news. It looks horrible out there."

I looked out onto the yard. The rain was coming down in sheets and it was so dark at eleven a.m. that I had all the lights on. "It's not so bad."

"Is something wrong, Eve? You don't sound good." Three thousand miles away and she could still tell that something was up.

"Mom, things have changed between me and Lorne. I've realized that I don't love him anymore."

There was silence on the other end of the line.

"Mom? Are you still there?"

My mother's voice was stiff, hard. "I'm here."

"I can't pretend any longer."

"Poor Lorne."

"He didn't seem too bad when I spoke to him. He said he'd see me in court."

"He loves you so much. He must be in shock."

"He's fine." I could feel myself starting to get angry. "He's got all his friends and family around. Everyone is in Toronto."

"That's true," my mother conceded. "So when are *you* coming home?"

"That's not what I meant."

"You can stay with me as long as you want."

"I'm not coming home, mom."

"You'll have to support yourself now, you know. It won't be like it was with Lorne. He treated you like a little princess."

I heard Sasha whimpering in the mudroom. "I'm really sorry, mom, but I have to go now. The dog has to go out."

"Don't tell me you bought a dog. You don't even know how to take care of yourself."

"She's not mine," I said, hoping to calm her down. "I'm house-sitting. To save money."

But once my mom was on the worry track, it was impossible to get her off. "I don't believe you've thought this thing through properly, Eve. Just think about what you're throwing away."

I imagined our house, the car, my walk-in closet filled with clothes and shoes. And then I thought of Lorne, pictured him shoved headfirst into a dumpster, and felt an immense sense of relief.

Sasha whimpered again.

"I have to take the dog out. I think she has to go to the bathroom."

"I wish you'd come to your senses and come home. I'm sure Lorne would still take you back."

As she said it, I knew immediately that going back to Toronto was the last thing I wanted. In that moment I decided I would stay on Green and be one with the quirky people. They would be my new family.

"I'll call you soon, mom. I promise."

"Don't do anything crazy. You know how you can be."

I hung up, put on my boots and raincoat, picked up Sasha, and carried her down the back steps. The rain had eased and I could see the sky lightening through the filigreed cedar boughs. I tried to stand Sasha up, but her hind legs were useless and just slid out from under her. The ground was wet and I didn't want to lay her in the mud, so I ended up squatting down behind her and holding her back legs up with my hands. She managed to crane her neck around and look toward me with her metallic, cataract-clouded eyes. I think she appreciated what I was trying to do, but it was hard to tell.

When she had finished, I carried her back inside. I refilled her food and water bowls, but she lay back down right away. She didn't seem hungry. I went back outside to fetch kindling and logs for the fire, which I put down in the living room. As I began to ball up sheets of newspaper from a basket beside the woodstove, I reviewed Jeff's fire-lighting instructions in my mind.

I took my time constructing a teepee of kindling over the paper, and then readied a pile of bigger sticks to feed the fire when it was time for the larger logs to go in. It took a couple of matches to get the paper going, but in a few minutes the fire was burning pretty well; fat flames licked the wooden teepee, and I could feel little fingers of warmth reaching out into the room. The cheerful blaze seemed like a good omen to me, an affirmation that everything was going to work out all right after all.

I watched the flames, enjoying the warmth and the sound of the crackling wood. After about half an hour of daydreaming, it occurred to me that I should do something memorable to ritualize the end of my marriage—something I could think back on later as the official beginning of my new life. I went through a cardboard box I'd brought with me and took out a couple of photos of me and Lorne skiing at Mont Blanc the previous Christmas, plus a postcard I'd written to him a few days before New Year's and never sent, and five or six poems I'd been working on for a while but could never get right. I also added a used sanitary napkin to the pile: a bizarre gesture to some, perhaps, but in my mind the symbolism was perfect. Blood and death. Beginnings and endings. Thank God I left him before I got pregnant.

My idea was to burn everything up. To incinerate my past life and all its falsity with a purifying fire that would make space for the new me to emerge like a phoenix from the ashes. But something was missing. I needed some kind of formal prayer to ritualize and bless the moment. I was raised on Friday night blessings and synagogue-directed prayers, and I figured some well-chosen words would really help to symbolize the transition.

I scanned my hosts' bookshelves for inspiration and lucked out. There, right beside a dog-eared copy of *Slaughtering Chickens for Fun and Profit* was a more useful book: *Helpful Spells for Modern Witches* by Eagle MoonRay. I scanned the table of contents and flipped to the chapter on "Spells for Self-Protection and Security."

The book said that all I had to do was follow the four simple instructions below in order to feel an immediate sense of inner security and self-protection.

Sasha whimpered again. It was cold in the mudroom, so I lifted her out and brought her closer to the fire. With the old dog settled in front of the woodstove, I dug out my bathrobe from the suitcase. It was a voluminous purple velour affair with large sleeves and a hood: just the right accessory for a ritual of this sort. I went back to the book.

1. Light a few candles.
2. Call on the four directions.
3. Say the prayer that's written in this book.
4. Repeat the prayer until you believe it.

I found some candles in a kitchen cupboard, lit them, and placed them on the floor on both sides of me. I wasn't quite sure what the book meant by calling on the four directions, so I just turned around and at each quarter-turn called out, "North," "South," "East," and "West," in both English and French, because that seemed more inclusive. Then I faced the stove, raised one arm in a kind of I-am-evoking-the-Great-Spirit pose, and started in on the prayer.

I am a child of the universe.
She fills me with her protective spirit.
I will be safe from accidents,
Injuries, sickness and death.
All is well, all is well, all is well.

I said the prayer a couple of times until I had it memorized. Then I stoked the fire with the poker. It didn't yet look impressive enough for my purposes, so I added some more logs, opened up the flue all the way, and waited for the wood to catch. I poked the fire again, shoved in my collection of mementos—including the used feminine hygiene product—and slammed the door fast because I was afraid of getting ashes on the floor.

At first, nothing happened. I looked over at Sasha, my adopted animal companion, for inspiration. But she appeared to be asleep. I decided to keep on praying.

> I am a child of the universe.
> She fills me with her protective spirit.
> I will be safe from accidents,
> Injuries, sickness and death.
> All is well, all is well, all is well.

I was swaying around the room in a witchy, emerging-goddess kind of way to get more into the mood when the edge of my bathrobe got a little too close to a candle and caught on fire.

As I was putting out the flames on my robe, the photographs, postcards, and poems finally caught fire in the woodstove. Okay, okay, I thought, I've put the fire on my robe out. I'll simply ignore the stench of singed purple velour and keep right on praying.

I took a moment to meditate on the flames that were licking up the inside of the stove. The fire was a metaphor for my own purification. It marked the necessary destruction of my past life that would allow for a new beginning, a beginning of my own creation. I imagined that by lighting that fire and saying the prayer, I was in fact incarnating the Goddess Kali, the mother of birth and death, who creates and also destroys. I swayed a little closer to the woodstove. The fire was really burning now, but strangely, the menstrual pad was still intact.

As I leaned in to get a closer look, there was a sudden blinding flash of light. The needle for the chimney thermostat—the one Jeff had told me to keep at Medium—swung wildly to the right and into the Extreme Danger zone. The inside of the stove was now a solid ball of flame. The handle on the door was too hot to touch, and I didn't know what else to do, so I just kept on praying.

> I am a child of the universe.
> She fills me with her protective spirit.

The stovepipe started shaking. Smoke poured out of it, and flames leapt out through the cracks on top of the stove. The thermostat needle read Nuclear Holocaust. I screamed:

> I will be safe from fire, fire, FIRE!!

I grabbed the fire extinguisher with one hand, and with the other, a small, fringed couch pillow to protect my hand as I yanked open the stove door. The wall of heat almost knocked me over. There were flames everywhere. I aimed the nozzle directly into the inferno, adopted my best Bruce Willis stance and pulled the trigger. White foam shot out with an impressive *whoosh* and expanded to fill the stove completely, then billowed out the door and onto the floor. In a matter of seconds the fire was out.

The room was suddenly quiet. I watched as a mushroom cloud of fire-extinguisher carcinogens drifted languidly up from the woodstove to rest gently against the ceiling.

When I put the extinguisher down, my hands were shaking and my heart was pounding so hard it was difficult to breathe. The living room was covered in ash and the room was hazy with smoke.

"My marriage is over," I croaked. "All is well, all is well, all is well."

I was just starting to clean up the mess when I realized that at some point during the "ritual," Sasha had taken her last breath.

So my mother was right after all. Without someone to watch out for me, I was sure to do something crazy and irresponsible. It was obvious that I was incapable of looking after myself.

The smells of extinguisher fumes and recently deceased dog were too much for me. I opened some windows, took off my robe, put on my boots, and went outside. The air was better out there. The sky was clear and I could see a crescent moon peeking out from behind the clouds. I needed to walk for a while, to clear my head, but all I could think about was how stupid I'd been, how I was going to be the laughingstock of the whole island, and how I might as well beg Lorne to take me back right now because my only other option was to spend the rest of my life living with my mother.

By the time I got back to the house I'd stopped crying, but I was still feeling terrible. When I walked in the door, the phone was ringing. I tried not to look at Sasha or the mess around the woodstove, and prayed it wasn't Jeff and Paula calling to check on their house or their beloved family pet. I figured the Goddess owed me that much at least.

"Hello, Eve?" I recognized the breathy voice on the other end of the line right away. It was Isis, Green Island's resident astrologer. I'd met her a couple of times at the Gas Bar Café.

"Hi Isis. Jeff and Paula aren't here."

"I know that."

Of course she did. Everyone knew everything about everybody on Green Island. That was exactly why I had to get on the next ferry, before I could see my failure reflected on the faces of the strangers I'd been stupid enough to think would one day be my new family. Her next sentence caught me off guard.

"I was wondering if you'd like to participate in a little ritual I'm organizing."

The word "ritual" made my stomach churn. Was it possible that she already knew what I'd done in Jeff and Paula's house? Was a hidden webcam broadcasting the whole sorry affair into the Gas Bar Café? Or did her astrological powers involve some kind of psychic element?

"Ritual?" I stammered. "Ah, well, actually I'm not really familiar...."

"I'll be leading it, of course," Isis reassured me. "I just finished a Wiccan correspondence course."

"It's really nice of you to invite me," I said, and I meant it. It was just too bad that the invitation had come too late. I'd already blown any chance at making friends on Green Island.

"We're going up to Stanton Park. Elliot Dale's started developing up there and he's going to cut down a whole stand of

Garry oak. I thought you'd be interested, since I heard you like to walk out there."

"I really appreciate the invitation, Isis. But I'm afraid I'll be leaving Green Island sooner than I had expected. I have to go back to Toronto."

Then I found myself telling Isis the whole story about the ritual and the inferno and Sasha dying and me being sure that everyone on the island was going to revile and despise me forever.

Isis laughed. "Are you kidding? Things are so boring around here in January that you're going to be the toast of the Gas Bar Café for weeks."

"What?"

"Listen, Eve," Isis said. "I'm sure you've noticed that pretty much everyone around here is slightly odd. Almost burning down the first place you housesit and probably causing the death of the family dog while doing a pagan ritual is kind of like your initiation into life on Green Island. It means you're just as crazy as the rest of us."

"But what about Jeff and Paula and the kids?"

"They'll be fine," Isis assured me. "Sasha's been ready to pass on for months, and Jeff would have put her down himself if he wasn't such a softie. He's a Libra rising, and you know how they are."

"Uh-huh," I said, though I had no idea what she meant. Still, I was starting to feel better. And I had noticed that pretty much everybody on Green was a little strange, albeit in a good way. That was part of what had attracted me to the island in the first place. "You really think it will be okay?"

"I guarantee it. So, can I count on you for the ritual?"

"Sure," I said. "It's for a good cause and it actually sounds like fun. Just don't let me near the matches."

Isis laughed. "I'll keep that in mind."

"One more thing," I said. "I think I know how to clean up the mess in the living room, but what should I do about Sasha?"

"What's your time, date, and place of birth?"

It seemed irrelevant to me, but I wasn't going to question the logic of someone who was starting to make me feel like I belonged on Green. "One-fifty in the afternoon on December 23, 1973. Toronto, Canada."

I heard Isis tapping away at a computer keyboard. "Very interesting," she said. "You're such a capable person." She'd obviously never spoken to my mother.

"So what should I do about Sasha?"

"I don't have to tell you that, Eve. You're a Capricorn with Taurus rising. You'll figure it out all on your own."

I wasn't feeling so sure about that when I hung up the phone, but whatever Isis saw in my chart that day must have been true, because by the time the living room was tidied up, I'd figured out what to do with the dog's body.

First, I took an old towel from the bathroom and lifted her onto it. Then I went into the mudroom and moved things around in the big freezer. It was easy enough to fit Sasha inside after that. I was relieved that her eyes were closed and she seemed to be at peace.

I couldn't just put the towel over her head and close the freezer door without saying anything, so I decided to repeat the only prayer I knew by heart. I shortened it a bit so it made more sense.

> You are a child of the universe.
> She fills you with her protective spirit.
> All is well, all is well, all is well.

B.A. Markus is a self-proclaimed bicoastal Canadian who wishes she could live in the heart of the BC rainforest and the urban jungle of Montreal at the same time. When she's not writing or teaching, she has a penchant for performing rituals of her own creation that usually involve setting something on fire.

Do you have a Great Story?

If you enjoyed this collection of stories and feel you have an outrageous, funny or inspirational tale that you would like to share about cottage country, we would love to hear from you. Our only rules are that your story must feature some unusual, illuminating or humorous twist to it, and that it's a (mostly) true anecdote.

Although we've already published eight volumes in our humor series, we are still hoping to publish more books in the genre. So if you have a great story, please send it to us. You don't have to be a professional writer. We look forward to hearing from anybody who has a great yarn to spin.

To obtain more detailed submission guidelines, please visit Summit Studios online at:

www.summitstudios.biz

Please submit stories or story proposals by e-mail or snail mail to:

SUMMIT STUDIOS
3022 Washington Ave.
Victoria, British Columbia V9A 1P6

E-mail: submissions@summitstudios.biz

We look forward to hearing from you.

Acknowledgements

A very special thanks to my wife, Stacey, who has a love for great stories. Without her unconditional support and her belief in my dream to found a publishing company, it would not have been possible to share these stories with you.

A big thanks to Curtis Foreman for his help with the proofreading and to Kirk Seton for a fantastic book design. They are both top-notch professionals.

Thanks to David Banks for a great cover illustration. I appreciated his insistence on getting all the smallest details right.

Thanks to my friends and family members who have offered their ideas, support, and critical feedback as this book has taken shape.

And finally, thanks to the many storytellers who have contributed their tales to this book. Their willingness to share means that we're all a little richer.

Other Titles by Matt Jackson

Mugged by a Moose

Edited by Matt Jackson

Is a bad day spent outside really better than a good day at the office? This collection of twenty-three short stories aims to answer that question.

Humor/Travel • Softcover • 216 pages
$19.95 • ISBN 9780973467130

Canadian Bestseller

"It's like Chicken Soup for the Funny Bone."
- The Kitchener-Waterloo Record

I Sold My Gold Tooth for Gas Money

Edited by Matt Jackson

Alternately laugh, cringe and giggle as twenty-six travel writers find themselves in some bizarre and unexpected situations.

Humour/Travel • Softcover • 216 pages
$19.95 • ISBN 9780973467147

Never Trust a Smiling Bear

Edited by Matt Jackson

The fifth volume in our bestselling humour series, where thirty-one writers serve up another helping of preposterous travel and outdoor tales.

Humour/Travel • Softcover • 216 pages
$19.95 • ISBN 9780973467185

The Canada Chronicles:
A Four-year Hitchhiking Odyssey

Written by Matt Jackson

Join the author on a four-year hitchhiking journey across Canada as he logs almost 30,000 kilometers, takes more than 25,000 photographs and meets hundreds of interesting characters from every corner of the country.

Adventure/Travel • Softcover
384 pages • 60 color photographs
$25.00 • ISBN 9780973467123

Canadian Bestseller and Winner of the 2005 IPPY Award

for Best North American Travel Memoir!

"Jackson's humor and charm shine throughout his storytelling."
- Canadian Geographic Magazine

A Beaver is Eating My Canoe

Edited by Matt Jackson

Another collection of wacky, funny, and inspiring tales from the far side of beyond, written by twenty-five free-spirited wanderers.

Humor/Travel • Softcover • 224 pages
$19.95 • ISBN 9780973467161

Canadian Bestseller

"Matt Jackson knows a funny travel story when he hears one."
- The Sarnia Observer

A Bear Stole My Fishing Boat

Edited by Matt Jackson

Traveling is not for the timid of heart. What can go wrong often does, as twenty-six travel-hardened writers relate in this book.

Humor/Travel • Softcover • 216 pages
$19.95 • ISBN 9780973467178

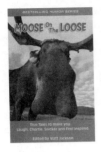

Moose on the Loose

Edited by Matt Jackson

The sixth volume in our bestselling travel and outdoor humor series, featuring twenty-six writers with stories that are outrageous, quirky, and downright hilarious.

Humour/Travel • Softcover • 224 pages
$19.95 • ISBN 9780986685606

Mob Hit on My Grandmother's Dog

Edited by Matt Jackson

A collection of thirty-three hilarious tales about animals. There are stories about domestic pets, tales about interactions with wild animals, as well as a few stories from the farm.

Humour/Travel • Softcover • 216 pages
$19.95 • ISBN 9780986685637

About Matt Jackson

A graduate of Wilfrid Laurier's Business Administration program in Waterloo, Canada, Matt Jackson was lured away from the corporate world by the thrill of adventure journalism while still a university student. He is now an author, editor, photojournalist and professional speaker, and is the president of Summit Studios, a publishing company specializing in books about travel and the outdoors.

Matt's first book, *The Canada Chronicles: A Four-year Hitchhiking Odyssey*, is a Canadian bestseller and won the IPPY award for best North American travel memoir in 2004. His work has also been featured in more than two dozen popular magazines including *Canadian Geographic, Backpacker, Canoe & Kayak, Explore,* and *BBC Wildlife*.

He lives with his wife Stacey and daughter Louise in Victoria, BC, where they spend as much time hiking and kayaking as possible.